LIFE AND MINISTRY OF THE MESSIAH

DISCOVERY GUIDE

That the World May Know® with Ray Vander Laan

LIFE AND MINISTRY OF THE MESSIAH

—————— 8 LESSONS ON ——————

Learning the Faith of Jesus

DISCOVERY GUIDE

EXPERIENCE THE BIBLE IN HISTORICAL CONTEXT™
Ray Vander Laan
with Stephen and Amanda Sorenson

CONTENTS

INTRODUCTION

Because God speaks to us through the Scriptures, studying them is a rewarding experience. Most of the inspired human authors of the Bible, as well as those to whom the words were originally given, were Jews living in the ancient Near East. God's words and actions spoke to them with such power, clarity, and purpose that they wrote them down and carefully preserved them as an authoritative body of literature.

God's use of human servants in revealing himself resulted in writings that clearly bear the stamp of time and place. The message of the Scriptures is, of course, eternal and unchanging — but the circumstances and conditions of the people of the Bible are unique to their times. Consequently, we most clearly understand God's truth when we know the cultural context within which he spoke and acted and the perception of the people with whom he communicated.

This does not mean that God's revelation is unclear if we don't know the cultural context. Rather, by learning how to think and approach life as Abraham, Moses, Ruth, Esther, and Paul did, modern Christians will deepen their appreciation of God's Word. To fully apply the message of the Bible to our lives, we must enter the world of the Bible and familiarize ourselves with its culture.

That is the purpose of this study. The events and characters of the Bible will be presented in their original settings. Although the DVD segments offer the latest archaeological research, this series is not intended to be a definitive cultural and geographical study of the lands of the Bible. No original scientific discoveries are revealed here. The purpose of this study is to help us better understand God's revealed mission for our lives by enabling us to hear and see his words in their original context.

Understanding the World of the Bible

More than 3,800 years ago, God spoke to his servant Abraham: "Go, walk through the length and breadth of the land, for I am giving it to you" (Genesis 13:17). From the outset, God's choice of a Hebrew nomad to begin his plan of salvation (that is still unfolding) was linked to the selection of a specific land where his redemptive work would begin. The nature of God's covenant relationship with his people demanded a place where their faith could be exercised and displayed to all nations so that the world would know of *Yahweh*, the true and faithful God.

In the Old Testament, God promised to protect and provide for the Hebrews. He began by giving them Canaan — a beautiful, fertile land where he would shower his blessings upon them. To possess this land, however, the Israelites had to live obediently before God. The Hebrew Scriptures repeatedly link Israel's obedience to God to the nation's continued possession of Canaan, just as they link its disobedience to the punishment of exile (Leviticus 18:24 – 28). When the Israelites were exiled from the Promised Land (2 Kings 18:11), they did not experience God's blessings. Only when they possessed the land did they know the fullness of God's promises.

By New Testament times, the Jewish people had been removed from the Promised Land by the Babylonians due to Israel's failure to live obediently before God (Jeremiah 25:4 – 11). The exile lasted seventy years, but its impact upon God's people was astounding. New patterns of worship developed, and scribes and experts in God's law shaped the new commitment to be faithful to him. The prophets predicted the appearance of a Messiah like King David who would revive the kingdom of the Hebrew people.

Even the Promised Land itself had changed, becoming home to many groups of people whose religious practices, moral values, and lifestyles conflicted with those of the Jews. The land that had been the nation of Judah was called "Palestine" or "Judea" (which means Jewish). The Romans had divided the land into several provinces: Judea, Samaria, and Galilee (the three main divisions during Jesus' time); Gaulanitis, the Decapolis, and Perea (east of the Jordan River); and Idumaea (Edom) and Nabatea (in the south). These further divisions of Israel added to the rich historical and cultural background that God had prepared for the coming of Jesus and the beginning of his church.

Living as God's witnesses took on added difficulty as Greek, Roman, and Samaritan worldviews mingled with that of the Jews. But the mission of God's people did not change. They were still to live so that *the world may know that our God is the true God*.

Our Purpose

Biblical writers assumed that their readers were familiar with the geography of the ancient Near East. Today, unfortunately, many Christians do not have even a basic geographical knowledge of the region. This study is designed to help solve that problem. We will be studying the people and events of the Bible in their geographical and historical contexts. Once we know the who, what, and where of a Bible story, we will be able to understand the why. By deepening our understanding of God's Word, we will be able to strengthen our relationship with him.

Western Christianity tends to spiritualize the faith of the people of the Bible. Modern Christians do not always do justice to God's desire that his people live faithfully for him in specific places, influencing the cultures around them by their words and actions. Instead of seeing the places to which God called his people as crossroads from which to influence the world, we focus on the glorious destination to which we are traveling as we ignore the world around us. We are focused on the destination, not the journey. We have unconsciously separated our walk with God from our responsibility to the world in which he has placed us.

In one sense, our earthly experience is simply preparation for an eternity in the new "Promised Land." Preoccupation with this idea, however, distorts the mission God has set for us. That mission is the same one he gave to the Israelites: to live obediently *within* the world so that through us, *the world may know that our God is the one true God*.

IN THE SHADOW OF HEROD

Herod the Great was king of Israel when Jesus was born. A ruthless and powerful king, he ruled from 37 BC until his death in 4 BC and controlled more territory than almost any previous king of the Jews. Herod is especially remembered for his magnificent building programs and his relentless suppression of all resistance — real or imagined. No matter how many potential enemies he crushed, he never felt secure in his realm and especially feared Cleopatra of Egypt. So he built a series of fortress-palaces to provide an escape route between his palace in Jerusalem and his ancestral homeland of Edom, which at that time was called Idumaea. From Jerusalem he could travel fewer than ten miles south to the safety of the Herodion, then about thirty miles to the cliff fortress of Masada, and finally the fifty miles to the safety of Idumaea.

The Herodion was a spectacular complex that symbolized Herod's visionary genius, power, and splendor. Built on a high hill, the Herodion was the third largest palace in the ancient world. Its buildings covered about forty-five acres surrounded by another two hundred acres of palace grounds. The walls of the upper palace stood about ninety feet tall with about half of that height covered by a steep rampart. One of the four massive defensive towers of the fortress extended high above these walls. The expansive lower palace at the base of the cone-shaped hill included elaborate halls and guest rooms, a terrace more than one thousand feet long, and a swimming pool (140 by 200 feet) surrounded by colonnades and a beautiful garden.

Many significant biblical sites are near the Herodion. A few miles to the north and west lies Bethlehem, and just beyond are the Judea

Mountains. Nearby are the hills where Jacob buried Rachel, the route Naomi and Ruth traveled from Moab, the fields owned by Boaz in which Ruth gleaned, the valley where Goliath died, and the place where Samuel anointed David as king of Israel. To the east is the Judea Wilderness, where shepherds grazed their flocks on the green pastures David described. In the distance, one can even see the Dead Sea and mountains of Moab.

Herod clearly intended his magnificent building projects to demonstrate his power and establish a lasting reputation for himself. The Herodion dominated the landscape and could be seen from Jerusalem — nearly ten miles north. As the sun rose and set, the Herodion literally cast its shadow across the surrounding towns. In a similar way, the personality and power of Herod cast a shadow across the landscape of Israel's history and people.

King Herod seemed to possess all power, magnificence, and glory. But during his reign, God brought together two vastly different kings — Jesus and Herod — to fulfill his purposes. Generations earlier Rebekah, the wife of Abraham's son, Isaac, conceived twins. "Two nations are in your womb," the Lord had told her, "and two peoples from within you will be separated; one people will be stronger than the other, and the older will serve the younger" (Genesis 25:23). Esau, the older son, founded Edom; Herod was one of his descendants. Jacob, the younger son, founded Israel; Jesus was one of his descendants.

Conflict between the descendants of Esau and Jacob had been predicted by Balaam: "A star will come out of Jacob; a scepter will rise out of Israel.... Edom will be conquered; ... but Israel will grow strong" (Numbers 24:17 – 18). Later Malachi prophesied, "I have loved Jacob, but Esau I have hated, and I have turned his mountains into a wasteland and left his inheritance to the desert jackals" (Malachi 1:2 – 3). So the Jews knew that even though Herod was their king, someday the line of Jacob would overpower the line of Esau.

No matter how strong and glorious Herod appeared to be, the baby in Bethlehem's manger represented true power. Today, Herod's buildings lie in ruins, and most people remember him only as the king who killed innocent babies while trying to kill the infant Jesus.

Whereas Herod made his mark on the world and then was gone, Jesus didn't leave a single building as a legacy. No one is exactly sure where he was born or died. Yet his passing changed the world forever. Jesus the Messiah, the Lord of heaven and earth, triumphed over all evil — even death! Today he lives! His kingdom has no end, and he will return to conquer all earthly powers.

Opening Thoughts (4 minutes)

The Very Words of God

> *After Jesus was born in Bethlehem of Judea, during the time of King Herod, Magi from the east came to Jerusalem and asked, "Where is the one who has been born king of the Jews? We saw his star in the east and have come to worship him." When King Herod heard this he was disturbed, and all Jerusalem with him.*
>
> Matthew 2:1 – 3

Think About It

One of the dramas we see played out every day in the world around us is our human striving to be "first," to be the most powerful, to be recognized as the best, to be the strongest, to be the richest. It was no different during the days of Jesus. But there is a greater power at work than the power we see exerted in this world.

Which situations in the Bible can you recall in which what appeared to be weak and powerless defeated that which appeared to be stronger and more powerful? What thoughts and feelings do these situations bring to mind as you consider the forces of evil at work in our world today? How can we know who wields the real power?

DVD Teaching Notes (18 minutes)

The Herodion in its setting

Israel and Edom: a history of conflict

Herod the Edomite versus Jesus the King of kings

DVD Discussion (7 minutes)

1. Which details about the Herodion impressed you the most?

Given the Herodion's size, purpose, and proximity to Bethlehem, what insight do you gain into why Joseph left in the middle of the night when he took Mary and Jesus to Egypt?

2. What are some of the contrasts between King Herod and Jesus the Messiah that stand out to you?

As you consider the contrasts in power between Herod and Jesus, what insights do you gain into God's perspective on power and his faithfulness in fulfilling his promises?

3. In what ways has this video changed your view of the faith that was required for Jews in Jesus' day, who lived under the harsh rule of Herod (and later his successors), to believe that Jesus truly was the Messiah?

PROFILE OF A FORTRESS
The Awesome Herodion

- Was located on a hilltop at the edge of the Judea Wilderness to provide a safe haven for Herod in the event he needed to flee Jerusalem.

- Had walls rising more than forty-five feet above the hilltop, with one watchtower rising an additional sixty feet or more, and could be seen from Jerusalem about ten miles away.

REMAINS OF THE HERODION RISE LIKE A VOLCANIC CONE ABOVE THE WILDERNESS PASTURES EAST OF THE JUDEAN HILLS

- Was built about thirty years before Jesus' birth near the site of Herod's battlefield victory over the Hasmonaeans, which earned him the Roman nomination to be the earthly king of the Jews.

- Overshadowed Bethlehem, about three miles away, where Jesus, the almighty King, was born.

- Was often passed by shepherds (such as those who came to see the baby Jesus) and farmers who lived in Bethlehem—a small town of at most several hundred people. Bethlehem had fertile farmland and was close to the wilderness where shepherds kept their flocks.

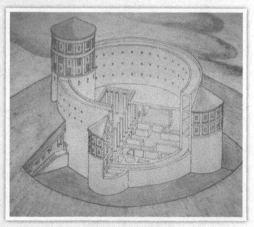

CUTAWAY DRAWING REVEALS THE INTERIOR STRUCTURE OF THE HERODION

The Upper Palace

- Had double cylindrical walls about fifteen feet apart with an outside diameter of nearly 220 feet. Between the walls were seven stories of apartments, chambers, and storage rooms. Herod covered the lower four stories with steep walls of packed dirt, creating the unique, volcanic-cone shape.

RUINS OF THE UPPER PALACE OF THE HERODION TODAY

- Was protected by smaller defensive towers on the south, north, and west that extended outside the cylindrical structure. The enormous eastern tower was fifty-five feet in diameter, more than 120 feet tall, and provided royal apartments for King Herod and his family.
- Included a glorious bath complex that featured a vaulted caldarium (hot bath), tepidarium (warm bath), and frigidarium (cold bath) — each of which had floors decorated with mosaics. Herod brought water from more than three miles away through aqueducts and stored it in cisterns at the base of the fortress-palace.
- Could accommodate many guests in its large, roofed reception hall that had colored plaster walls. During the Jewish revolts long after Herod's death, the Zealots made the reception hall into a synagogue.
- Had an open-air garden with columns on three sides and a niche at each end for statues.
- Was entered by a 300-step stairway on the outside of the mountain followed by a 200-foot-long tunnel that led into the fortress.

The Lower Palace

- Consisted of a complex of buildings and a pool at the foot of the mountain. The pool — one of the largest in the ancient world — was ten feet

continued on next page . . .

**THE GRAND SCALE OF THE LOWER PALACE OF
THE HERODION IS EVIDENT EVEN TODAY**

deep, 140 feet long, 200 feet wide, and was surrounded by colonnaded gardens—quite a sight given that the water came via aqueduct. On an island more than forty feet in diameter in the middle of the pool stood a colonnaded circular building in which Herod and guests could relax in complete privacy.

- Contained a huge building complex between the pool and the upper fortress, with more than 400 feet of elaborate halls and guest rooms. In front was a terrace more than 1,000 feet long.
- Presumably holds the tomb of Herod. Though this largest of the fortress structures has not yet been completely excavated, renowned Herod scholar Ehud Netzer appears to have unearthed the remains of Herod's tomb—the grave, sarcophagus, and mausoleum—on the east slope of the Herodion. Netzer began excavating at the Herodion in 1972 and made this discovery as excavations began on the palace slope in 2006. The tomb was hidden because the site's mausoleum was mostly demolished in ancient times. Only a large platform of white dressed stone remained buried in the soil on the side of the hill. Although hundreds of fragments of red-colored limestone believed to be from Herod's highly ornamented eight-foot sarcophagus have been found around the site, no inscriptions

have been discovered so far. Netzer believes the Zealots broke into the tomb during one of the Jewish revolts and demolished the tomb and the sarcophagus. They may have even scattered the remains of the king in defiance of his pagan ways. This appears to confirm a significant irony. Herod, the Edomite, the descendant of Esau, one of the most powerful kings of Israel's history, was buried in the immediate vicinity of Bethlehem where Jesus, descendant of Jacob, helpless infant in a manger, was born king of the Jews … and the entire universe (Matthew 2:1). Once again the human trappings of power mislead us, for it is " 'not by might nor by power, but by my Spirit,' says the LORD Almighty" (Zechariah 4:6).

NEWLY EXPOSED EDGE OF PODIUM OF WHAT IS BELIEVED TO BE HEROD'S TOMB (BROKEN PIECE OF FRIEZE IS ORIGINALLY PART OF THE MAUSOLEUM ROOF)

Small Group Bible Discovery and Discussion (19 minutes)

A Contrast Between Two Kings

It's amazing to realize that Jesus, the self-sacrificing King of the universe, was born in the shadow of the palace-fortress of Herod the Great, the renowned, self-glorifying king who killed anyone he thought might stand in his way — including members of his family, close advisors, and the innocent babies of Bethlehem. Jesus and

Herod, who for a short time lived just a few miles apart, had conflicting worldviews and held vastly different types of power. Herod had all the power, wealth, and glory that the world could offer. Jesus had nothing of worldly value, but he had the power to overcome every evil (including that of Herod).

1. Read Matthew 2:1 – 18, which portrays some of the intrigue and conflict that took place when Jesus was born as king of the Jews during the reign of King Herod, who was Rome's choice as ruler of the Jews.

   a. What do you learn about King Herod's power, what he feared, and how far he would go to eliminate potential rivals, specifically Jesus?

   b. How would you describe the contrasts between Jesus' and Herod's position, destiny, and impact on other people that lie "beneath the surface" in Matthew's account?

   c. The wise men of the east met with Herod face-to-face and personally witnessed the material evidence of his greatness, yet they continued on to Bethlehem (with the great Herodion clearly in view) to worship the infant king, Jesus. What do you think about the faith that inspired their journey, prompted them to bring gifts for

him, and led them to refuse to reveal the location of the
child to Herod?

2. Given the nature of Herod's rule, why was the shepherds'
   visit to Bethlehem to see Jesus such an act of faith? (See Luke
   2:8–18.)

3. What do you think motivated Herod the Great, and in contrast, what motivated Jesus—the Messiah, the King of the
   universe—to do what he did on earth? (See John 4:34; 5:30;
   10:10–11, 14.)

4. By bringing Jesus and King Herod—two kings who
   couldn't have been more different morally, spiritually,
   materially—together at the same time in history, what do
   you think God was revealing about how he works? About
   his kingdom?

PROFILES IN CONTRAST

Jesus	Herod the Great
Placed in a manger	Lived in magnificent palaces
Appeared as a weak and powerless baby	Appeared to have great strength and power
Had no earthly status but really had it all — eternal power, glory, authority, etc.	Had great earthly status, but lacked eternal status
Lived to honor his Father and fulfill God's purposes	Lived to glorify himself and fulfill his own purposes
Built a kingdom of people for the glory of God so that others would know Yahweh is truly God	Built a kingdom of glorious buildings in order to honor himself and maintain good relations with Rome
Dedicated to serving others	Self-serving
Had ultimate authority and still does (Ephesians 1:18 – 22)	Had only limited earthly authority
Died in agony on the cross to remove the sins of humankind	Died in agony, hated by his family, after ordering one of his sons to be executed
The Messiah from Jacob's lineage who overcame all evil but was never accepted as King of the Jews	The Edomite whose reign violated God's rules (Deuteronomy 17:15) and was never accepted by the Jews

Faith Lesson (6 minutes)

Herod had all the power, wealth, strength, and glory that his worldly position could offer. Jesus, the King of the universe, had nothing of that sort to demonstrate his position. Read Luke 2:8 – 20, which sheds light on the great step of faith that was required for the Jews of Jesus' day — including the shepherds mentioned in this passage — to believe that the baby Jesus in the manger was the Messiah, the Lord of heaven and earth.

1. What earthly king would send such an important and glorious announcement of his coming to mere shepherds?

If you had been a resident of Bethlehem when Jesus was born, what might you have thought if the shepherds had told you about the divine announcement of the Savior's coming?

Why would it have been frightening for the events of Jesus' birth to occur, as they did, in plain view of the Herodion, which was such a powerful symbol of Herod's might and glory?

If you had lived in Bethlehem, who would you have believed was more powerful and worthy of your honor and allegiance — Jesus or King Herod? Why?

2. What kind of faith did it take for the shepherds to respond as they did to the news of the Messiah's birth?

Why was it risky for them to tell other people that a new king, the King of heaven and earth, had been born?

What would Herod likely have done to the shepherds if he had discovered they actually visited and worshiped another king?

In what ways are the risks you face in worshiping Jesus and telling others about him similar to or different from the ones that people during his lifetime on earth were asked to take?

Closing (1 minute)

Read Luke 2:15 – 18 aloud: "When the angels had left them and gone into heaven, the shepherds said to one another, 'Let's go to Bethlehem and see this thing that has happened, which the Lord has told us about.' So they hurried off and found Mary and Joseph, and the baby, who was lying in the manger. When they had seen him, they spread the word concerning what had been told them about this child, and all who heard it were amazed at what the shepherds said to them."

Spend time in prayer, asking God to help you remember that no matter how pervasive and powerful evil appears to be, God's power is even greater. Thank him for the work he is still accomplishing in the world and ask him to help you walk in faith and obey him in all things.

Memorize

When the angels had left them and gone into heaven, the shepherds said to one another, "Let's go to Bethlehem and see this thing that has happened, which the Lord has told us about." So they hurried off and found Mary and Joseph, and the baby, who was lying in the manger. When they had seen him, they spread the word concerning what had been told them about this child, and all who heard it were amazed at what the shepherds said to them.

Luke 2:15 – 18

Understanding the World in Which Jesus Lived

In-Depth Personal Study Sessions

Day One | Israel and Edom: Nations in Conflict

The Very Words of God

> *Moses sent messengers from Kadesh to the king of Edom, saying: ... "Please let us pass through your country. We will not go through any field or vineyard, or drink water from any well. We will travel along the king's highway and not turn to the right or to the left until we have passed through your territory."*
>
> *But Edom answered: "You may not pass through here; if you try, we will march out and attack you with the sword."*
>
> Numbers 20:14–18

Bible Discovery

A Tale of Two Brothers

The conflict between Jacob and Esau, twin grandsons of Abraham, began before they were born and led to long-term tension between the powerful nations they founded. At times, these nations tolerated each other; more often they fought each other. History reveals that Herod the Great, the king who tried to kill Jesus the Messiah (a descendant of Jacob), came from the nation Esau founded.

1. Genesis tells the story of Jacob and Esau, the grandsons of Abraham. What do you learn about the nature of their relationship from each of the following passages?

   Genesis 25:21 – 26

Genesis 25:27 – 34

Genesis 27:1 – 10, 22 – 35

2. Where did the descendants of Jacob and Esau settle? Locate these areas on the map on page 28. (See Genesis 35:1, 6 – 7, 9 – 13; 36:1 – 9.)

3. When Esau begged for a blessing from his father, how did Isaac answer him? (See Genesis 27:34 – 40.)

How was Isaac's answer reflected in the prophecy of Balaam regarding Jacob's people — the Israelites — and Esau's people — the Edomites? (See Numbers 24:15 – 19.)

In what ways has Isaac's answer been reflected in the history of relationships between Israel and Edom? (See Numbers 20:14 – 21; 1 Kings 11:14 – 25; 2 Kings 8:20 – 22.)

What did God, through his prophets, say the descendants of Jacob and Esau would experience because of Edom's long-standing bitterness against Israel? (See Ezekiel 35:1 – 15; Amos 1:11 – 12; 9:11 – 12; Obadiah 8 – 18.)

4. History reveals that Herod the Great came from Idumaea (what Edom was called at the time of Jesus). How does what Jesus accomplished on earth during Herod's reign fit with the blessings given to Jacob and Esau and the prophecies about Israel and Edom?

DATA FILE
The Edom Connection

Esau's descendants settled in the mountainous country of Edom that lay to the east and south of the Dead Sea. They were to have a kindred relationship with Israel through Esau, and the third generation of Edomites could, in fact, be received into Israel (Deuteronomy 23:7 – 8). Yet the history of Jacob and Esau and their descendants is a history of deception and conflict.

- When the Israelites wanted to pass through the land of Edom on their way to the Promised Land, the king of Edom refused their request and threatened to attack them if they tried (Numbers 20:14 – 18).
- During the reign of the kings of Israel, conflict between Israel and Edom continued. The Edomites at times were Israel's allies and at other times allied themselves with Israel's enemies (1 Kings 11:14 – 17; 2 Kings 3:4 – 9; 8:20 – 22; 2 Chronicles 20:1 – 12, 22 – 24).
- The bitter conflict between these nations continued to escalate. When Israel was finally destroyed and carried off to Babylon, Edom not only did nothing to relieve their suffering but added to it. God promised the destruction of Edom because of their hostility toward their brothers (Ezekiel 35:1 – 15; Obadiah 8 – 18).

continued on next page . . .

By the time Jesus was born, the area or province of Edom was known by its Greek name, Idumea, and had been greatly extended toward the north and west. This was due to the influence of Herod's father, Antipater, and the Roman decision of the provincial boundaries. As Herod's father was ruler of Idumaea, and his mother was a Nabatean from Petra, the capital city of Edom, Herod clearly would have been recognized as a descendant of Esau. Jesus, on the other hand, was a descendant of Jacob, and people knew that when the Messiah came, the line of Jacob would conquer the line of Esau.

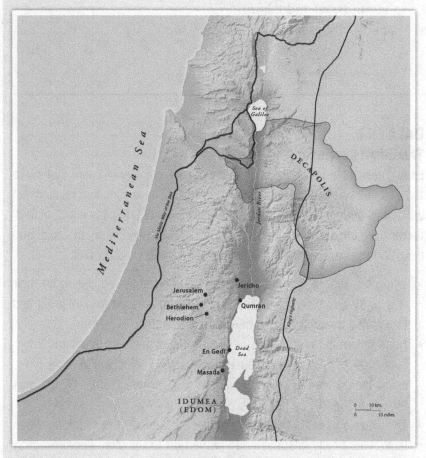

TOPOGRAPHY OF ISRAEL: NEW TESTAMENT

Reflection

The deceit between Jacob and Esau grew into a bitter, complicated struggle between the nations of Edom and Israel. No wonder God abhors the sin of deceit. While it's easy for us to point fingers at Rebekah and her son, Jacob, for deceiving Isaac and Esau, we must remember that we are not immune from the temptation and consequences of deceit.

> What are some of the ways — even "small" ways — in which we practice deceit?

> In what ways is deceit dangerous to us? To others?

Ephesians 4:31 reminds us of what bitterness, such as that which grew from the deceit between Jacob and Esau, does when it is not dealt with properly through confession and forgiveness.

> In what way(s) has deceit hurt you or someone close to you?

> Who do you need to forgive so that bitterness will not cause you to stumble?

Memorize

> *Get rid of all bitterness, rage and anger, brawling and slander, along with every form of malice. Be kind and compassionate to one another, forgiving each other, just as in Christ God forgave you.*
>
> *Ephesians 4:31 – 32*

Day Two | Bethlehem — Small but Significant

The Very Words of God

> But you, Bethlehem Ephrathah, though you are small among the clans of
> Judah, out of you will come for me one who will be ruler over Israel, whose
> origins are from of old, from ancient times.

Micah 5:2

Bible Discovery

God Chose Bethlehem to Fulfill His Purposes

Despite Bethlehem's small size, some of the events that took place
there thousands of years ago still impact the world today. Bethlehem's role in history provides hints that for a long time God had
been accomplishing his work in this unassuming town which, when
Jesus was born, was overshadowed by the great Herodion.

1. Look at the map of Israel on page 28. Note Bethlehem's location in relationship to Jerusalem, the Herodion, the Judea
   Mountains, the Judea Wilderness, Moab, and Edom (Idumaea). Which occupations did Bethlehem's unique location
   at the border between the mountains and the wilderness
   enable its people to have?

2. For which events that caused great grief is Bethlehem
   known, and what gift from Bethlehem would remove all
   tears? (See Genesis 35:14 – 19; Jeremiah 31:15 – 17; Matthew
   2:16 – 18.)

3. What place do King David and Ruth, the Moabitess, have in common, and for what common purpose did God include them in his plan? (See Ruth 1:1 – 6, 22; 1 Samuel 16:1 – 3, 12 – 13; Matthew 1:1, 5 – 6, 17.)

4. About seven hundred years before Jesus was born, what did the prophet Micah say would happen in Bethlehem? (See Micah 5:2.)

Why, then, was it important for Jesus to be born in Bethlehem? (See Luke 1:30 – 33; 2:1 – 7.)

Reflection

When Jesus was born, the contrasts between Bethlehem and the Herodion could not have been greater. One seemed insignificant — a small town located between the terraced farmland of the Judea Mountains and the rugged wilderness where shepherds found pasture for their flocks. The other was a massive monument to Herod's power — a magnificent structure that literally towered over the countryside, casting its shadow over the landscape. Yet God used Bethlehem to accomplish his eternal purposes.

As you think about how God specifically chose Bethlehem to be Jesus' birthplace, what can you — if you are an obedient follower of Jesus — believe about his plans for you?

What comparisons might you draw between what eventually happened to the Herodion and what will happen to people today who trust in their own power, resources, and glory to create "monuments" to themselves?

What does the fact that Jesus was born in a small town populated mainly by shepherds and farmers reveal about God's willingness to use seemingly insignificant locations and ordinary people to change the world?

Just as God, long ago, set in motion a plan for Jesus to be born in Bethlehem in the lineage of David, God is still at work in our world today — in small communities as well as large cities. How can you discover what God is doing in your culture and community — and participate with him in doing it?

DATA FILE
The Works of a Master Builder
Herod the Great's visionary building programs, ingenious development of trade with other countries, and advancement of his nation's interests are remarkable. His magnificent building projects helped to strengthen his relationship with Rome and fulfill his desire to be recognized as the greatest builder and king the Jews ever had.

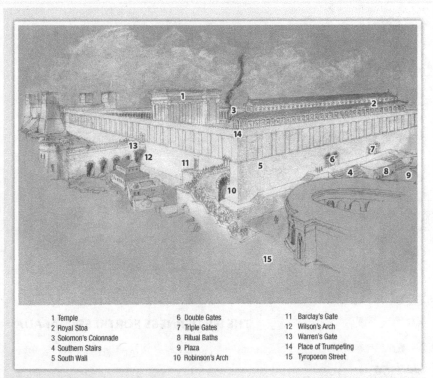

1 Temple	6 Double Gates	11 Barclay's Gate
2 Royal Stoa	7 Triple Gates	12 Wilson's Arch
3 Solomon's Colonnade	8 Ritual Baths	13 Warren's Gate
4 Southern Stairs	9 Plaza	14 Place of Trumpeting
5 South Wall	10 Robinson's Arch	15 Tyropoeon Street

THE TEMPLE MOUNT

Jerusalem

Herod rebuilt the temple out of marble and gold. The building was taller than a fifteen-story building, and its foundation included limestone blocks weighing more than 500 tons. On the western hill of the city, he built a spectacular palace complex that included reception halls, apartments, fountains, gardens, baths, and a fortress for his personal guards. He also built a Greek theater and hippodrome, paved the streets, and installed sewers.

Masada

Perched atop a plateau in the Judea Wilderness, this fortress was one of the wonders of the ancient world. A spectacular palace suspended from one end of the plateau, luxurious hot and cold baths, mosaic floors, swimming pools, huge storehouses, barracks for soldiers, and cisterns holding millions of gallons of water helped to make this hot, dry wilderness outpost bearable for its occupants.

continued on next page . . .

THE WILDERNESS FORTRESS, MASADA

Jericho

This palace was built on both sides of a wadi (a dry, deep riverbed), and a bridge spanned the riverbed. One wing contained a huge, marble-floored hall where Herod received guests. Next to it were peristyle gardens, dining halls, and a complete Roman bath. Across the wadi, another large building housed baths, a swimming pool, and gardens.

Caesarea

Needing contact with the Roman world for its military support and trade opportunities, Herod built Caesarea into one of the most amazing seaports of the ancient world. Founded in 22 BC, the city housed a large theater, amphi-theater, hippodrome, a massive temple to Augustus, and — of course — an elaborate seaside palace. Much of the city was built with imported marble, and the city had an elaborate sewer system that was cleansed by the sea.

The city's real glory, however, lay in its forty-acre, man-made harbor. A light-house guided ships that brought Roman legions, marble, granite, and the Hellenistic culture into the region. From the harbor, ships also carried spices, olive oil, grain, and—most important—the gospel to the far reaches of the world.

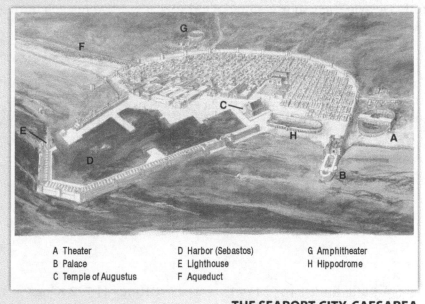

A Theater   D Harbor (Sebastos)   G Amphitheater
B Palace   E Lighthouse   H Hippodrome
C Temple of Augustus   F Aqueduct

THE SEAPORT CITY, CAESAREA

Day Three | God's Plan for the Birth of the Savior Unfolds

The Very Words of God

The plans of the LORD stand firm forever, the purposes of his heart through all generations.

Psalm 33:11

Bible Discovery

God Used All Kinds of People to Help Accomplish Jesus' Birth

Just as Bethlehem was a small, seemingly unlikely place for God to choose as the birthplace of the Messiah, God also used seemingly unlikely, imperfect people to accomplish his plan of redemption. Some of them had suffered life-changing loss and sorrow; others had grown up in idol-worshiping cultures; yet another had been a prostitute. Despite their shortcomings, God was at work — in each of their lives as well as in his plans for the birth of the Savior.

1. Read the following portions of Scripture and note the flaws and strengths of the people involved.

   Tamar: Genesis 38:6 – 19, 24 – 26

   Rahab: Joshua 2:1 – 14, 6:22 – 25

   Ruth: Ruth 1:1 – 6, 15 – 17; 4:9 – 17; 1 Kings 11:7; 2 Kings 3:26 – 27

   David: 1 Samuel 16:1 – 13

   Bathsheba: 2 Samuel 11:1 – 5, 14 – 17, 26 – 27; 12:7 – 19, 24 – 25

2. What do each of these people have in common? (See Matthew 1:1 – 6, 17.)

3. Of all the people God could have chosen, why do you think he selected these particular people to have a role in bringing about the birth of the Messiah?

4. We often have strong expectations of the kinds of people God can and cannot use to accomplish his work. For example, Ruth, Naomi's daughter-in-law, was reared in Moab, a pagan country near Israel.

    a. What do the following verses reveal about Ruth's cultural background that might cause concern about her usefulness in participating in God's plan? (See Genesis 19:30 – 38; 1 Kings 11:7; 2 Kings 3:26 – 27.)

    b. Why did Ruth return to Bethlehem with Naomi, and what does this reveal about her faith? (See Ruth 1:15 – 18.)

    c. After recognizing Ruth's faithful commitment to him, what did God work out for her, and what were the consequences? (See Ruth 4:9 – 16; Matthew 1:6 – 17.)

DID YOU KNOW?
Worlds Apart, But Still within View

The Dead Sea, which is barely ten miles east of Bethlehem, lies at the bottom of the Great Rift Valley. The mountains of Moab, the homeland of Ruth, rise above the eastern shores of the Dead Sea. Naomi fled to Moab with her husband and sons to escape a famine in Israel. So when Ruth went with Naomi to Bethlehem, she probably moved fewer than twenty miles. On a clear day, Ruth could even have seen the mountains of her homeland. What a significant, although not extensive, trip that turned out to be!

**THE WILDERNESS
EAST OF BETHLEHEM**

Reflection

It's easy for us to judge people according to where they live, how they relate to other people, whether or not they have committed certain sins, or how "successful" they are according to our earthly standards. It's also easy for us to discount the extent to which God can use people who "don't seem to measure up" to accomplish his will. So from a human standpoint, it's amazing that God placed some of the people he has in the lineage of Jesus. What this reveals about God and his work in our lives is important for us to think about.

How does the fact that God used Ruth, who grew up in Moab — a nation that began in incest, worshiped false gods, and participated in child sacrifice — relate to the times when we feel we have sinned too greatly or too often to be of any service to God?

Do you sometimes feel as if the failures in your past will keep God from using you in a significant way? How might the stories of people God has chosen to use in the past help you better understand his redemptive work in your life?

Why do you think God often uses "undeserving people" by the world's standards to accomplish great things for his kingdom?

How can you know for sure that God loves you and will fulfill his purpose through you?

Memorize

It is God who works in you to will and to act according to his good purpose.

Philippians 2:13

Day Four | Jesus Christ Is King

The Very Words of God

Therefore God exalted him [Jesus] to the highest place and gave him the name that is above every name, that at the name of Jesus every knee should bow, in heaven and on earth and under the earth, and every tongue confess that Jesus Christ is Lord, to the glory of God the Father.

Philippians 2:9 – 11

Bible Discovery

God Sends a King of His Choosing

King Herod ruled with unmatched power and authority. He lived in amazing splendor and luxury, enjoying the best life had to offer. Everything he did was intended to glorify himself and magnify his own power. In contrast, Jesus came to earth with none of the usual trappings of greatness. He was born to unknown parents in a small town that was literally overshadowed by the Herodion, and he lived what seemed to be an ordinary life on earth. But make no mistake about the fact that Jesus is king. He is simply king of a different kind of kingdom — an eternal kingdom where his power is unlimited and where true greatness bears little resemblance to earthly ideas of greatness.

1. What did the prophets say about the kind of king God would send to his people?

    Isaiah 9:2 - 7

    Isaiah 11:1 - 5

    Micah 5:2 - 5

2. King Herod was intensely motivated to bring honor and glory to himself. In contrast, what motivated Jesus to do what he did while he was here on earth? (See John 13:3 - 5, 12 - 17; 2 Corinthians 8:9; Philippians 2:6 - 8.)

3. The power King Herod wielded was highly visible. He had incredible political power that was backed by Rome. He commissioned massive construction projects. He simply said the words, and his enemies were executed. In contrast, what kind of power did Jesus demonstrate?

   Matthew 8:23 – 27

   Matthew 10:1

   Luke 5:17 – 26

   John 10:25 – 28

4. King Herod left behind a record of brutal enforcement of his power and a legacy of monumental building projects that today lie in ruins. In contrast, what did Jesus accomplish during his days on earth? What is the legacy of the King of kings? (See Matthew 20:25 – 28; Hebrews 2:9, 14 – 15; 1 John 2:2.)

5. Whereas King Herod sought the exultation of men and women during his life on earth, Jesus sought to fulfill his Father's will. Afterward, what kind of exultation did Jesus receive? (See Mark 16:19; Philippians 2:8 – 11.)

KEY DATES FOR ISRAEL'S HISTORY OF RULERS

586 BC	Babylonian captivity of Judah
538 BC	Return to Israel
332 BC	Alexander the Great conquers Israel
330–198 BC	Rule of Hellenistic Ptolemies over the Jews
198–167 BC	Oppression under Hellenistic Seleucids
167 BC	Maccabee revolt
167–63 BC	Hasmonaean kingdom
37 BC	Herod the Great begins his reign
c. 6 BC	Jesus' birth
4 BC	Herod the Great dies
c. AD 30	Jesus is crucified
AD 66–73	First Jewish revolt
AD 70	Roman destruction of Jerusalem during first Jewish revolt
AD 73	Masada falls
AD 131–135	Bar Kochba revolt (second Jewish revolt)

Reflection

So great are the contrasts between what we tend to honor in kings and leaders and what God values that we should give careful thought as to what these differences might mean in how we live and seek to serve God every day.

Describe in your own words the character, strength, and power that God honors in a king.

As you consider the kind of King God chose for his people, what are the implications for your life as you consider what Jesus has done, and is willing to do, for you?

To what extent do you trust in your own power, wisdom, and accomplishments as opposed to trusting in God's power, wisdom, and guidance?

How thankful are you for the King whom God has sent to be Lord of your life?

How deeply do you praise him?

What do you do to bring honor to Jesus' name so that other people will know who he is?

Memorize

I heard every creature in heaven and on earth and under the earth and on the sea, and all that is in them, singing: "To him who sits on the throne and to the Lamb be praise and honor and glory and power, for ever and ever!"

Revelation 5:13

Day Five | Living by the Power of the King

The Very Words of God

The LORD will fulfill his purpose for me; your love, O LORD, endures forever.

Psalm 138:8

Bible Discovery

God Is Pleased to Accomplish His Work through Us

God calls everyone who claims to be a follower of Jesus to desire to obey and accomplish his will. He is willing and able to use each of us, no matter how flawed, weak, or insignificant we may be in the eyes of the world. All God needs in order to use us in significant ways is our willing heart.

1. What difference does our earthly appearance or status make in our ability to fulfill God's purposes well? (See 1 Samuel 16:1, 6 – 7.)

2. Even when circumstances threaten to prevent God's plan from happening, who is still in control? (See Genesis 45:4 – 8.)

3. When God calls us to accomplish his work, the task is often greater than we can imagine doing. What is the source of our ability to fulfill what God sets before us, and how do we become equipped to accomplish it? (See 2 Samuel

7:8 – 9; 1 Corinthians 1:26 – 29; 2 Corinthians 9:8; Hebrews 13:20 – 21.)

Reflection

Today, we are asked to believe that Jesus is King, no matter how overwhelming Wall Street's power, the government's control, Hollywood's morals, and the evils of pornography, hunger, AIDS, and racism appear to be.

To what extent do you dare to live as if God is greater than any evil you face in life and culture?

How confident are you that God can use you in significant ways, just as he has used many other people to bring about his purposes on earth?

In what way(s) are you paying more attention to outward appearances rather than demonstrating faith in God?

Which of your beliefs concerning God and yourself may not line up with who he really is, how he works, and his plan for you?

What or who are the "Herods" of your life — the powers of evil that seem so strong and glorious or that seem more attractive and important than following Jesus?

Which specific actions will you dare to take because you trust that the power of Jesus the Messiah within you is greater than any evil you will face, and that God is in control even when it appears otherwise?

MY ROCK AND MY FORTRESS

The ruins of Masada, one of Herod the Great's spectacular fortress-palaces, stand high above the Dead Sea in the mountainous Judea Wilderness. Today, this fortress is remembered not so much as a testimony to Herod's greatness, but because it is a testimony to the long-standing desire of the Jews for freedom and political independence. That desire influenced nearly every aspect of life for the Jewish people during the time of Jesus.

From the time Herod the Great was made king in 37 BC, the Jews seethed under Roman rule. After Herod's death in 4 BC, things got worse. Weary of Roman oppression, the Jews became increasingly nationalistic and eager to escape Roman domination. That is part of the reason they were so eager for the coming of the Messiah; they assumed that he would deliver them from the Romans. No wonder some of them were disappointed in Jesus who came to bring a different kind of deliverance.

Eventually, in AD 66, a social and political explosion sent shock waves throughout Israel. Jews in Caesarea — Herod the Great's marvelous port city from which early Christians left to take the gospel to the world — objected to a Gentile sacrifice offered near the synagogue entrance. This set off mass killings and riots throughout Israel and the Roman Empire. For a short time the Zealots gained control, but Roman troops poured into Caesarea ... Galilee ... Gamla ... to crush the Zealot movement. Fighting continued until the Romans destroyed Jerusalem, its temple, and its people in AD 70.

Despite the best of Rome's efforts, some Jewish Zealots (967 people, including women and children, according to the Jewish historian Josephus) escaped to Masada, a cliffside fortress overlooking the Rift

Valley between the Negev Wilderness and the Dead Sea. Because Herod the Great built Masada as a refuge in case he ever had to flee Jerusalem, the Zealots had everything they needed: fifteen huge storehouses of food, weapons, and supplies; cisterns holding a million or more gallons of water; swimming pools; living quarters; and a virtually impregnable mountaintop location. According to Josephus, Herod had stockpiled enough materials to supply thousands of men for up to ten years. The Zealots settled in, studied the Torah, and waited.

When the Zealots' occupation of Masada became known, Rome's Tenth Legion established eight camps around Masada. They had few options: a frontal assault up the narrow pathway, leaving, or doing a siege. After building a wall more than two miles long completely around Masada, the Legion spent seven months building an enormous siege ramp against the western side of the mountain. To accomplish these massive projects, they used the labor of thousands of captured Jews.

After completing the ramp, the Legion used its enormous battering ram to smash a hole in Masada's wall. But inside, the Zealots had built an adjoining wall of timbers and filled the space in between with dirt, which absorbed the pounding of the battering ram. In response, the Romans set the timber wall on fire.

As the fire burned, the Zealots faced a tragic choice. Their commander, Eleazar, said in effect, "We Zealots have always known that to live in slavery is wrong. We should not be slaves to anyone. God did not create us to be slaves. The most important thing in the life of a person is the right to be free from oppression." He then emphasized how cruelly the Romans would treat anyone they captured.

Having spent nine years fighting the Romans, the Zealots had seen their nation and culture destroyed, their holy temple desecrated, and their families and friends killed, enslaved, and/or tortured. As they thought about God and what they believed life to be, they made their choice. Believing that it was wrong to owe allegiance to anyone or anything other than God, they put their belief into action. They burned everything of value except weapons and food (so the

Legion couldn't say they died of starvation or lack of weaponry), and chose to die by their own hands rather than surrender. Only two old women and five children survived.

Opening Thoughts (4 minutes)

The Very Words of God

> *The Lord is my rock, my fortress and my deliverer; my God is my rock, in whom I take refuge. He is my shield and the horn of my salvation, my stronghold.*
>
> Psalm 18:2

Think About It

All of us have someone or something that we count on to get us through times of trouble. It may be a person or financial resources, our attitude or ability. Perhaps it is a belief about ourselves or the world in which we live.

When you face tough times, what do you view as your personal backup plan that provides feelings of safety or security for you? When you read in Scripture about God being our *fortress* in times of trouble, what does that metaphor communicate to you?

DVD Teaching Notes (21 minutes)

Wilderness fortresses

David's Masada

Herod's Masada

The Zealots' Masada

The Zealots' commitment—more than words

DVD Discussion (7 minutes)

1. Now that you have seen a glimpse of the Judea Wilderness, how does it differ from what you imagined it would be?

    What dangers and hazards, safety and hope did the wilderness offer?

    What do you think it was like for David and his men to hide out in the wilderness?

2. In what ways might the type of wilderness experience David had encourage you to depend on God as your fortress, and in what ways might it tempt you to depend on yourself?

3. Which features of the fortress and palace Herod built at Masada most impressed you?

DID YOU KNOW?

David wrote these words: "I love you, O LORD, my strength. The LORD is my rock, my fortress and my deliverer" (Psalm 18:1–2). The word transliterated "fortress" here is really a rendering of a Hebrew word that can be translated *masada* in English. The psalmist recognized the solid, unmovable, unshakable characteristics of the Lord God. He looked around at the formidable strength of his rugged, rocky, mountainous world and thought, *That is what God is to me. He is a rock and fortress in which I can trust.*

Small Group Bible Discovery and Discussion (17 minutes)

A Fortress in the Wilderness

Much of Israel is quite rocky, and the Judea Wilderness between the mountains and the Dead Sea is no exception. The familiar presence and characteristics of rock, combined with the Jews' practice of describing spiritual reality in terms of concrete images from the world in which they lived, led to the frequent description of God as their "rock." A "fortress," a safe place to hide from enemies and find rest and peace in the midst of a harsh environment, was another familiar wilderness image that the Jews often used to describe God's role in their lives. Let's consider how various people may have viewed God as their rock and fortress in the wilderness.

1. According to 1 Samuel 23:14, 24–29, where did David hide when King Saul was seeking to kill him? (On the map on page 53, locate the areas described.)

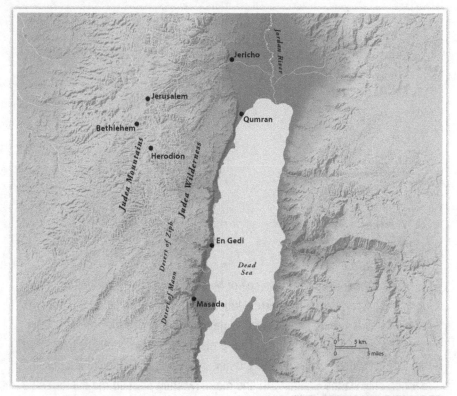

THE JUDEA WILDERNESS

2. Although David found safe hiding places in wilderness strongholds in the vicinity of Masada, what did he consider to be his true protection? (See Psalm 18:1 – 2, 46 – 50; Psalm 71:1 – 3.)

What response did that protection inspire in David's heart? (See Psalm 63:1 – 7.)

3. Long after David sought refuge from King Saul, Herod the
    Great built the fortress-palace of Masada in the same wilder-
    ness area. In what ways did David and Herod view their pro-
    tection differently?

DATA FILE
The Wonders of Masada
Why Masada?

Herod built the fortress and palaces of Masada on a huge rock plateau overlooking the Dead Sea in the barren Judea Wilderness. The top of the plateau,
more than twenty-one acres in size, is nearly 1,300 feet above the sea. Obviously Masada's height provided great protection, but Herod also surrounded
the summit with a wall and thirty defensive towers. The fortress could be
reached only via the Snake Path, the main, twisting path on the eastern side

1 The Mountain   2 Northern Palace   3 Western Palace   4 Roman Bathhouse   5 Cistern   6 Storehouse

MASADA

of the mountain, and a path on the western side. Strong, heavily guarded gates protected each of these entrances into the fortress.

Although located in a desert wilderness, Masada was not far from hospitable areas. Herod could quickly leave Jerusalem and flee to Masada if the Jewish people revolted or if Herod's Roman master, Antony, gave Herod's domain to Cleopatra, his enemy to the south. Masada was also near Herod's homeland of Idumaea.

Masada's Palaces

The western palace served as Herod's main living quarters at Masada. Occupying more than 37,000 square feet, this building included royal apartments, bathrooms, a cold-water pool, and a large reception hall with magnificently decorated mosaic pavement. Nearby were servants' quarters, workshops, a huge kitchen, and three richly decorated palaces—probably for the families of Herod's wives, who did not get along.

Another palace, built into the northern end of the mountain, was known as the "hanging palace." The upper level of this remarkable building perched on top of the mountain, and the two lower levels were built into the cliff face below.

MASADA: NORTHERN PALACE

continued on next page . . .

MOSAIC

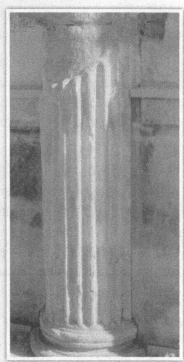

COLUMN

- The upper terrace featured lavish living quarters with mosaic floors, frescoed walls, and a semicircular balcony that offered spectacular views.
- The round, middle terrace had two concentric rows of columns that created a beautiful balcony for relaxation.
- The lower terrace, surrounded by low walls and columns with a roof in between, provided an open court inside a colonnade. A bathroom on its eastern side had mosaic floors. The great retaining walls that supported this level remain a testimony to the genius of Herod's engineers.

Water: Masada's Greatest Luxury

Despite its dry, wilderness location, Masada boasted one of the largest bathing complexes of its time. The largest room of the Roman-style bathhouse contained a hot bath (caldarium), which was much like a sauna. A warm bath (tepidarium) and cold bath (frigidarium) were adjacent. All of the baths were elegantly decorated with frescoes and mosaic floors. In addition, there were several swimming pools within the fortress. The elaborate bathing complexes and water supply reveal much about Herod's obsessive fears concerning safety and his craving for opulence and luxury.

To gather the water needed to supply such luxuries, Herod and his engineers created a brilliant water system. Masada was perched on a mountain plateau between two wadis that occasionally flooded when it rained in the mountains to the west. So Herod diverted some of the floodwater into twelve cisterns cut into the mountain. The cisterns could hold more than 1.5 million cubic feet of water—enough to sustain thousands of people for up to ten years! Water was bucketed up about 300 feet to the top of the plateau where it was stored in cisterns that could hold more than one million gallons. Thus Masada had an enormous supply of fresh water.

Masada's Storehouses

Fifteen storehouses, some more than sixty feet long and twelve feet wide, contained food, weapons, and other goods needed to provide security and luxury for Herod and his army. Some storerooms were filled with rows upon rows of amphorae (large pottery jars) containing olive oil, flour, wine, and other provisions.

STOREHOUSES OF MASADA

4. Long after Herod died, near the end of the first Jewish revolt, a group of Zealots took refuge in the wilderness fortress of Masada to escape the wrath of Rome. The Zealots passionately believed that it was wrong to owe allegiance to anything or anyone but God. What do you think about the way in which they carried out that belief, and how do you think they viewed God as their "rock" and "fortress"?

5. Although we may describe God's protection in different terms today, God is still the "rock" and "fortress" of his people. Read Matthew 6:25 – 33 aloud as a group, then discuss how Jesus might want to influence your efforts to protect and provide for yourself in your world.

Faith Lesson (5 minutes)

David counted on God to be his fortress in times of trouble. He trusted in God, his enduring rock. King Herod, on the other hand, trusted in Masada. He counted on the fortress to save him in times of trouble and trusted in his palaces and storehouses — the results of his own labor and abilities. Where we place our trust makes all the difference.

1. To what extent are you trusting God for security, protection, and strength, as David did? In what ways are you, like King Herod, trusting in the work of your own hands?

What difference does the object of your trust make in your sense of security? In your relationship with people around you? In your relationship with God?

What can happen, even today, when people place trust in their "masadas" instead of the living Messiah?

2. Think about a specific time in your life (or in the life of someone you know) when God became a "rock" and "fortress." In what ways did your understanding of life and your relationship with God change as a result?

3. In which practical ways are you depending on God to be your "rock" and "fortress" today?

How do you find the balance between trusting God to be your "rock" and "fortress," on the one hand, and on the other hand, using your *own* efforts to provide security and stability for yourself and other people?

Closing (1 minute)

Read Psalm 31:2 aloud: "Turn your ear to me, come quickly to my rescue; be my rock of refuge, a strong fortress to save me." Then pray, asking God to help you open your eyes and heart to the protection, strength, and freedom that he offers. Pray that you will, as David did, quickly turn to God as you live boldly for him. Ask God, too, for the strength and love to become a rock of encouragement, shelter, and strength for other people.

Memorize

> *Turn your ear to me, come quickly to my rescue; be my rock of refuge, a strong fortress to save me.*
>
> **Psalm 31:2**

Understanding the World in Which Jesus Lived

In-Depth Personal Study Sessions

Day One | Finding Safety in the Wilderness

The Very Words of God

> *Praise be to the* LORD *my Rock, who trains my hands for war, my fingers for battle. He is my loving God and my fortress, my stronghold and my deliverer, my shield, in whom I take refuge, who subdues peoples under me.*
>
> Psalm 144:1 – 2

Bible Discovery

What Did It Mean for God to Be David's Rock and Fortress?

David and his men often had to find safe hiding places in the wilderness. Although David knew the ways of the wilderness very well, he remained keenly aware that his wilderness skills, which had been honed during his years as a shepherd, were not the ultimate source of his security and protection. Neither did he rely on his renowned skills as a warrior and leader as his true safety net. In the heat of barren, dry, rugged landscape, David found safety and security in his God.

1. In Psalm 18:28 – 29 and 32 – 36, David uses a series of images to describe what God does for him. Given what you have learned about the geography and landscape of the Judea Wilderness near Masada, how do these images help you better understand David's appreciation for and dependence on God in his world? For example, how advantageous would it be to scale a wall in that wilderness? To have nimble, secure feet like a deer? To avoid a sprained ankle?

2. At times David fled to the wilderness because King Saul
    wanted to kill him. Imagine yourself in David's situation,
    having done nothing wrong, yet having to hide and survive
    in such a harsh environment. Then read Psalm 62:5 – 8. How
    did David view his difficulties and his hope differently from
    how you might tend to view things? What was most impor-
    tant to him?

3. What does Psalm 18:1 – 3 reveal about the kind of relation-
    ship David had with God?

    How important was David's obedience to God in that rela-
    tionship? (See Psalm 18:20 – 26.)

    How and why did God respond to David when David needed
    help? (See Psalm 18:16 – 19.)

Reflection

Today it's easy to view our "fortress" as being governmental authority, how much money we have accumulated, our status in the community, and so on. God, however, wants to be our fortress — the One
we count on, the One we trust to meet our needs, our *masada*.

How does the biblical picture of God being a fortress relate to
your life right now?

What hinders you from viewing God as your ultimate "fortress"?

Is it a lack of trust, a lack of knowledge of who God is, a lack of obedience, a lack of experience in depending on God?

What aspects of your life exert pressure on you to count on other things and people as your security?

What steps can you take to get to know the God that David knew, to build a relationship in which God is your true strength and hope in life?

Memorize

You are my hiding place; you will protect me from trouble and surround me with songs of deliverance.

Psalm 32:7

Day Two | The Lord Is Our Rock and Fortress

The Very Words of God

There is no one holy like the LORD; there is no one besides you; there is no Rock like our God.

1 Samuel 2:2

Bible Discovery

The Rock That Is Our God

The perception of God being like a "rock" probably began in the
desert terrain where the Israelites learned to trust God before they
entered the Promised Land. David frequently connected the image
of "rock" with Israel's God, and over time "rock" essentially became
a synonym for God. It was a powerful image that the people of
Jesus' day understood. To better understand its meaning for our
lives, we need to explore how it is used in God's Word.

1. When David was in the wilderness, to what did he attribute
   his safety? (See 2 Samuel 22:1 - 3.)

   How do we know that David clearly connected the image of
   a rock with Israel's God? (See 2 Samuel 22:47 - 50; 23:3 - 4.)

2. As you read the following passages, take note of what the
   image of God as a "rock" conveyed. Write in your own words
   the message and significance of the image.

Scripture Text	God as a "Rock"
Gen. 49:22 – 24	
Deut. 32:4	
Deut. 32:18	
Deut. 32:30 – 31	
1 Sam. 2:2	
Isa. 44:6 – 8	
1 Cor. 10:1 – 4	

Reflection

It's easy to *read* about God being a "rock" for David and the people of ancient Israel. It's another matter to understand what they were saying about the God represented by that image and to consider how we can discover and depend on him in the world in which we live.

Many passages of Scripture use the rock image to describe God's unfailing strength. When have you or someone you know relied on God's strength?

What happened?

Which images from your world would you use to describe the strength of God and how he uses it to help his people?

The "rock" image also conveys the idea of God's deliverance. In what ways did God deliver David from his trouble and suffering, and how does he deliver people today?

The "fortress" image often conveys God's protection. When have you or someone you know relied on God's protection?

What happened?

Which images from your world would you use to describe how God protects his people?

Can you sing, as David did when God delivered him from his enemies, that "The Lord is my rock, my fortress and my deliverer; my God is my rock, in whom I take refuge" (2 Samuel 22:2 – 3)? Is God the refuge in whom you trust? Why or why not?

Day Three | Longing for the Messiah

The Very Words of God

> *After the people saw the miraculous sign that Jesus did, they began to say, "Surely this is the Prophet who is to come into the world." Jesus, knowing that they intended to come and make him king by force, withdrew again to a mountain by himself.*
>
> **John 6:14 – 15**

Bible Discovery

Messianic Expectations Reach Their Peak

With generations of captivity behind them and Roman oppression a threat to daily life, the Jews of Jesus' day eagerly anticipated the Messiah's coming. They knew from the earliest Scriptures that he would usher in a new kingdom, and they looked forward to the changes they assumed he would make to their situation. Jesus came to earth as this time of intense messianic anticipation and conflict reached its peak. Committed to allegiance to God, and God alone, the Jewish Zealots had begun taking matters into their own hands. They were ready to put their commitment into action and rid their country of the hated Roman oppressors — even if it meant they would die for what they believed.

1. It's no wonder that the Jews were excited about the Messiah's coming. Consider what the ancient Scripture texts said about the Messiah. If you had been living at that time, what would you have looked forward to?

   Isaiah 9:1 – 2, 6 – 7; 62:11

   Jeremiah 23:5 – 6

   Micah 5:2

   Zechariah 9:9 – 10

2. When the Jewish people began to realize who Jesus was, how eager were some of them to establish him as their king? (See John 6:14 – 15.)

3. After Jesus' resurrection, he spent forty days teaching his
    disciples about the kingdom of God. What did his disciples
    ask him during this time, and what does their question
    reveal about their messianic expectations? (See Acts 1:1 – 6.)

4. Consider the events that took place in Gethsemane when
    Jesus was arrested. In each of the following gospel accounts,
    what evidence do you see of the disciples' understanding of
    the kingdom of God and their expectations for the Messiah?
    In contrast, what did Jesus have in mind?

The Gospel Account	The Disciples' Perception of God's Kingdom	The Kingdom of God as Jesus Knew It
Matt. 26:50 – 56		
Luke 22:47 – 52		
John 18:4 – 11		

Reflection

When we consider the volatile circumstances under which the Jews lived when Jesus came to earth, it's no wonder that people were longing for their Messiah to save them.

> In what ways had the prophecies about the Messiah prepared the Jews for Jesus' coming, and in what ways had their circumstances prepared them?

> If you had been a Jew living during Jesus' time, why would you have focused on the hope of the coming Messiah, and what would you have expected the Messiah to be like?

> How closely do you think your expectations would have matched what God was accomplishing? Do you think you would have been inclined to participate in the life of his kingdom, or would you have preferred to pursue the ways of a different type of kingdom?

> How important is it to *really* study the Bible and learn all you can about God and how to live according to the purposes and standards of his kingdom? How willing are you to give your allegiance to God alone and to live for him in your world?

WORTH OBSERVING
Jesus and the Jewish Revolts

Although Jesus was crucified by the Romans nearly forty years before the first Jewish revolt, he understood the decision the Jewish people had to make concerning their Messiah. At least one of his disciples, Simon, was a Zealot (Matthew 10:4), but the kingdom Jesus came to bring was not the kingdom of the Zealot or the sword (Matthew 26:51–52). Recognizing his people's patriotism, anger against the Romans, and desire for freedom, Jesus was careful not to trumpet his power. In fact, Jesus frequently commanded the people he healed not to tell anyone what he had done for them — possibly because people might misunderstand his role in light of the growing nationalistic climate (Matthew 8:1–4; 9:27–30; 12:15–16; Luke 8:51–56; Mark 1:40–44; 3:10–12; 5:38–43; 7:33–36). Even so, people often saw in Jesus a Davidic king, a military conqueror who would rescue them from the Romans (John 6:14–15; Acts 1:1–6).

Clearly, Jesus predicted the destruction that would result from the revolt (Matthew 24:1–2). His knowledge led him to weep as he described what would happen (Luke 19:41–44). Some Jews were looking for military solutions to their problems rather than spiritual ones, to a political messiah rather than the Lamb of God who came to take away the sins of the world. Jesus warned his followers not to participate in that method of bringing in God's kingdom. Whereas some Jews were seeking salvation through political and military might (which led to their destruction), Jesus taught and lived out completely different truths.

Today, the Jewish people finally have returned to the land they lost during the first and second Jewish revolts. Yet, even today the message of Jesus the Messiah is relevant: he alone is God's hope of peace.

Day Four | The King of the Jews Comes to His People

The Very Words of God

> *For to us a child is born, to us a son is given, and the government will be on his shoulders. And he will be called Wonderful Counselor, Mighty God, Everlasting Father, Prince of Peace. Of the increase of his government and peace there will be no end. He will reign on David's throne and over his kingdom, establishing and upholding it with justice and righteousness from that time on and forever.*
>
> Isaiah 9:6–7

Bible Discovery

A Different Kind of Messiah

After waiting for the promised Messiah for so long, most Jews of Jesus' day found it difficult to accept him for the king he was rather than the king they expected him to be. Some expected a military conqueror; others expected a political leader. In either case, most were certain their Messiah would deliver them from Roman domination. Sadly, most Jews rejected the Messiah because he was not what they expected.

1. Which words of John the Baptist might have alerted people to the fact that the Messiah would not necessarily be what they imagined him to be? (See John 1:29, 36.)

2. What do Matthew 10:2–4 and Acts 1:13 reveal about Simon, one of Jesus' disciples?

Considering the kind of Messiah Jesus was, why is this surprising?

What questions do you think might have gone through Simon's mind when Jesus taught as he did in Matthew 5:38 – 44 and John 18:36?

3. Since Jesus did not bring about political freedom, military peace, or overthrow existing kingdoms, what kind of freedom, peace, and kingdom did he come to offer? (See John 8:31; 14:19 – 21, 26 – 27; 16:33; 18:36 – 37.)

4. Jesus was obviously aware of the people's expectations for their Messiah, the growing nationalistic climate, and the fact that false messiahs were proclaiming messages of their own liking.

    a. What did Jesus frequently command people he taught and/or healed, and why do you think he did this? How was this in itself contrary to what people probably expected the Messiah to do? (See Matthew 8:1 – 4; 9:27 – 30; Mark 1:40 – 44; 5:38 – 43; Luke 8:51 – 56.)

    b. As he approached Jerusalem on what we call Palm Sunday, the people welcomed him with cheers. Why did their enthusiasm cause Jesus such deep grief? (See Luke 19:35 – 44.)

NOTE: Palm branches were a patriotic symbol for the Zealots, and "hosanna," meaning "Jahweh save us," was a request for God's deliverance that was used in Maccabee celebrations.

c. Why do you think so many Jews missed the message of peace Jesus offered and chose instead the course that led to Masada?

Reflection

Although some people of Jesus' day believed him to be the Messiah, many still wanted to make him into a military-political Messiah who would bring about freedom from Rome. Instead of listening to the kind of Messiah Jesus claimed to be, they tried to make him into something else — and missed the peace and salvation he offered.

Today, many people still try to make Jesus into someone other than who he is. They declare him to be a good man, for example, but vehemently deny his deity. What are some other illustrations of this?

In what way(s) have you tried to mold Jesus into someone he isn't? Why is that so easy to do in our culture where "truth," especially biblical truth, is questioned and often cast aside in deference to individual opinion and belief?

Think about the ruins of Masada and the Zealots' commitment. What insights do they offer concerning the vital importance of understanding and obeying the true gospel of Jesus, not one of our own making?

Memorize

Jesus said, "My kingdom is not of this world. If it were, my servants would fight to prevent my arrest by the Jews. But now my kingdom is from another place."

John 18:36

Day Five | David: Committed to God in All Circumstances

The Very Words of God

Those who know your name will trust in you, for you, LORD, have never forsaken those who seek you.

Psalm 9:10

Bible Discovery

Living for God, Even during Times of Trouble

David's time in the desert wilderness near Masada and En Gedi provides important lessons for us in learning to trust and depend on God, particularly during times of trouble. David's passionate commitment to God and his faithfulness in submitting to God's will in spite of harsh circumstances stand as a model to believers today who also face times of helplessness, loss, doubts, and other "wilderness" experiences.

THE JUDEA WILDERNESS

1. What was the reason God rejected Saul as king and chose David? (See 1 Samuel 13:9 – 14; 15:10 – 23; 16:1, 6 – 12.)

2. When David went up to fight against Goliath, what evidence do we see of his motivating passion in life? (See 1 Samuel 17:45 – 47.)

3. As David became famous, Saul grew jealous. As Saul's jealousy grew to hatred, he tried to kill David.

   a. What was it about their spiritual makeup that made Saul and David's responses predictable? (See 1 Samuel 18:6 – 15.)

b. David may have written Psalm 62 while Saul was pursuing him. How would you describe David's state of mind?
In what hope did he place his trust? (See Psalm 62:1 – 8.)

4. For each of the following passages, describe the provision
and hope that God gave to David in the wilderness.

2 Samuel 22:1 – 7

Psalm 18:1 – 6

Psalm 31:1 – 5, 9 – 13

Psalm 91:1 – 16

TRUSTING GOD IN THE MIDST OF HARDSHIP

A passionate desire to obey God does not mean a life free of hardship. In fact,
Jesus taught his disciples that following him would lead to even greater hardship (John 15:18 – 21). But we can be encouraged that those who have gone
before us have remained faithful to God in the midst of hardships similar to
the ones we face. Consider some of the hardships David faced, for example.
How much are they like the challenges you face?

Scripture Text	Hardships David Faced
1 Sam. 17:28 – 30	Sibling conflict
1 Sam. 18:8 – 11	Multiple attempts on his life
1 Sam. 21:10 – 15	Acted insane to save his life
1 Sam. 22:18 – 23	Grief and guilt when priests and a whole town died because of him
1 Sam. 20:17; 31:8 – 10; 2 Sam. 1:17 – 27	The death of his friend, Jonathan
2 Sam. 6:16, 20 – 23	Permanent estrangement from his wife, Michal

Reflection

Everyone experiences some degree of difficulty and hardship. We may not be pursued by a jealous, vengeful king or face the possibility of capture by a brutal conqueror. But we are likely to feel anxious, weak, lonely, inadequate, afraid, or ill-prepared when we face the challenges and injustices of life. The overriding question is, *How deeply rooted and passionate is our commitment to God? Is he the one in whom we will trust and place our confidence when "wilderness" times arise?*

What have you learned from David about counting on God during your "wilderness" experiences?

Why is faithful obedience to God such an important part of receiving his blessings?

What are some of the "pits," "storms," "floods," or other situations that have stretched you to the breaking point?

Where do you turn first when you face difficulties you can't handle?

Do you find it easy to turn to God and pour out your needs and deepest feelings to him? Why or why not?

Sometimes life is so challenging that we feel overwhelmed and wonder if God really does care about us. How can you know for sure that God is with you and listens to your prayers?

David sometimes relied on other people — to come alongside him, to go to battle with him, to provide for his needs. Which person(s) in your life has God provided for you — to model what it means to trust God and submit to his will and to provide practical help and guidance?

Memorize

Be at rest once more, O my soul, for the Lord has been good to you. For you, O Lord, have delivered my soul from death, my eyes from tears, my feet from stumbling, that I may walk before the Lord in the land of the living.

Psalm 116:7 – 9

THE TIME HAD FULLY COME

In 1947, Bedouins discovered the ancient Dead Sea Scrolls that had been hidden in caves surrounding the Essene community of Qumran. To some extent, these scrolls have revolutionized our understanding of the Bible. They have affirmed God's protection of his inspired Word, showing that Old Testament books have changed little through the centuries. And the scrolls have provided insight into the theological beliefs and expectations of people who lived during Jesus' time.

The Essenes also have helped us to see ways in which God prepared a movement of people who anticipated Jesus' coming, paved the way for his teachings, and were ready to follow him. Archaeological studies of the Essenes' community and their writings shed light on Paul's words: "But when the time had fully come, God sent his Son . . . to redeem" (Galatians 4:4-5). God sent the Messiah into a carefully prepared setting — the first-century Jewish culture — and the Essenes' role in shaping that culture shows us that God's redemptive plan began unfolding long before Jesus' birth.

The story of the Essenes began, in a sense, in 167 BC when the Jewish Hasmonaeans (Maccabees) overthrew their Greek rulers. For the first time in nearly 500 years, the Jews were independent. But the Hasmonaeans became as Hellenistic as the Greeks who had ruled before them. When they appointed an openly Hellenistic high priest, two separate groups of devout Jews — the Pharisees and the Essenes — formed to oppose Hasmonean authority in the temple. The Essenes were devout Jewish separatists who left the city and temple for periods of time in order to establish alternative — and in their minds, more holy — ways of worshiping and honoring Yahweh.

There were Essene communities in Galilee, Judea, and even Jerusalem, but most Essenes studied in Qumran, the community by the Dead Sea. Believing they had been called to isolate themselves from the spiritual darkness of Hellenistic society and live in right relationship with God, the Essenes sought to create a new system of purity. When the Messiah arrived — an event they believed was imminent — they wanted him to find people who were prepared to battle the forces of spiritual darkness and reestablish the true priesthood and true kingship of David.

Despite their physical isolation in the wilderness, the Essenes influenced the theological climate of the Jews for about 200 years. Using copper, leather, and parchment, Essene scribes wrote extensively about their lifestyle, the coming Messiah, and the exciting new age that would soon arrive. They wrote out nearly all of the books of the Old Testament and developed theological concepts and practices quite similar to those of early Christians. For example, they:

- Practiced a form of ritual cleansing by water that is similar to baptism.

- Used many words and phrases that later appeared in New Testament writings and a method of Scripture interpretation similar to one early Christians used.

- Established a communal lifestyle similar to that of early Christians.

- Believed in justification by faith.

- Called themselves the "New Israel" and thought of themselves as sons of spiritual light who were preparing the "way of the Lord" by obeying his truths and not compromising with evil.

- Believed that they were living at the end of an age and that two messiahs — a priest messiah (Son of the most high God) and a king messiah (who would arrive with power and authority to drive out the sons of spiritual darkness) — would soon appear.

An earthquake in 31 BC destroyed Qumran's buildings, and the community was abandoned until about 4 BC when Herod the Great died and his son, Archelaus, became ruler. In AD 68, Roman troops destroyed Qumran. Although the Essenes existed for only a couple centuries, they helped to prepare the way for God's plan of redemption, shaping the theological context so that Jesus' teaching could be understood more easily because of its similarity to existing beliefs. They stand as yet another reminder that our Christian faith is rooted in a long line of Jewish people and their heritage. Clearly, God had prepared a fertile seedbed in which to cultivate the new faith he would plant on earth.

Opening Thoughts (4 minutes)

The Very Words of God

> You were once darkness, but now you are light in the Lord. Live as children of light (for the fruit of the light consists in all goodness, righteousness and truth) and find out what pleases the Lord. Have nothing to do with the fruitless deeds of darkness, but rather expose them.
>
> *Ephesians 5:8 – 11*

Think About It

As Christians, we sometimes think that if we could just retreat from the distractions and temptations of life in the world, we could live a holy life.

What do you think are the possible benefits and drawbacks of retreating from the world in order to pursue holy living? Do you think it is possible for normal, ordinary people to live holy lives in the midst of a spiritually dark culture? Explain your viewpoint.

DVD Teaching Notes (18 minutes)

The Essenes

Their community

Their lifestyle and practices

Their beliefs

Their great contribution

Understanding God's work in history

DVD Discussion (7 minutes)

1. What new insights into the Dead Sea Scrolls and the faith of the Essene community at Qumran did you gain through this video?

   What impressed you about the level of commitment the Essenes demonstrated in their walk with God?

Biblical Books Recorded on the Dead Sea Scrolls	Number of Scrolls Found Per Book
The Psalms	36
Deuteronomy	29
Isaiah	21
Exodus	17
Genesis	15
Leviticus	13
Numbers	8

2. Why is it significant that the Essenes developed theological concepts and practices similar to those of the early Christians?

   Which beliefs and values of Christians today are similar to those of the Essenes?

What does it mean to you to realize how deeply rooted the Christian faith is in the beliefs and practices of the Jewish people and culture?

3. What is your response to God when you see how carefully he had been preparing his people for the Messiah's coming?

DATA FILE
The Dead Sea Scrolls: An Accidental Discovery

It was a typical day in the Judea Wilderness in 1947. Near an old ruin at the northern end of the Dead Sea that scholars later recognized as Qumran, a Bedouin shepherd rounded up stray goats at the foot of barren cliffs. He noticed a small opening to a cave, and when he threw a stone into the opening he heard the distinctive sound of pottery breaking. After telling two other family members about his discovery, he returned home with his goats.

THE CAVES OF QUMRAN

The next day, Mohammed edh Dhib squeezed into the cave, which was littered with broken pottery. Two of the ten intact jars contained a large scroll and two smaller ones, which the disappointed Mohammed showed to the other shepherds. Little did they know that they had just discovered incredible treasures—the book of Isaiah, the Manual of Discipline (describing Qumran community rules), and a commentary on the book of Habakkuk!

Mohammed hung the scrolls from his tent pole in a bag for several months, then sold them to an antiquities dealer named Kando in Bethlehem. Kando found the cave, located additional scrolls, and then—after showing them to church officials at Jerusalem's Syrian Orthodox Monastery of St. Mark's—sold the three original scrolls to a Jerusalem antiquities dealer named Samuel for less than one hundred dollars.

As word of the discovery spread, Professor E. L. Sukenik of the Hebrew University purchased Kando's additional scrolls. Meanwhile, Samuel had taken the three scrolls to the United States and advertised them in the *Wall Street Journal* on June 1, 1954. Dr. Sukenik's son, Yigael Yadin, happened to see the ad and, through a middleman, purchased the original find for $250,000 and presented the scrolls to the State of Israel. Today, they are in the Israel Museum in Jerusalem.

Bedouin from Mohammed edh Dhib's tribe soon located more caves near Qumran containing additional scrolls and thousands of scroll fragments. An official archaeological investigation was launched to examine the caves and the nearby ruins.

Known today as the Dead Sea Scrolls, scrolls (mostly scroll fragments) were found in at least eleven caves near the ruins of Qumran. Among the 600 scrolls represented, a few of which had been preserved in clay jars (the extremely dry climate aided in preservation), scholars have identified copies of all the books of the Old Testament except Esther; Jewish writings from other sources, such as the apocryphal book of Jubilees; and specific writings from the Qumran community that included Old Testament commentaries, liturgical writing such as hymns, and rules for community conduct.

continued on next page . . .

The most well-known scrolls include the nearly intact Isaiah scroll; the Copper Scroll that describes sixty-four locations where temple treasures were hidden (none of which have been found); the Habakkuk commentary in which the prophecies of God's judgment are applied to the Romans and those who resisted the Essenes' beliefs; and the Manual of Discipline describing the rules of the Essene community. One of the most significant archaeological finds of modern times, the Dead Sea Scrolls have:

- Profoundly affected our understanding of biblical texts.
- Provided striking insight into the theological and cultural setting of Jesus' life, the early church, and the history of Judaism.
- Provided fresh insight into our understanding and application of the Bible's message.
- Affirmed the accuracy of the Scriptures. (Until the Dead Sea discoveries, the oldest copies of the Hebrew Bible dated to approximately AD 1000. The scrolls take us back beyond 100 BC.) Scholars were amazed to find few differences between old and new texts—most involved spelling changes.

Truly, "All Scripture is God-breathed and is useful for teaching, rebuking, correcting and training in righteousness" (2 Timothy 3:16). Although a follower of God trusts the truth of the Bible by faith, the scrolls confirm that our faith in the Bible is fully supported by scholarly evidence.

AUTHOR'S NOTE: Scholarly debate continues as to whether the scrolls were written or used at Qumran, whether they were the product of the Essenes, and whether the Essenes actually lived at Qumran. The best evidence to date indicates that the Dead Sea Scrolls were the product of the Essenes and were written or collected at the Qumran settlement. The actual contents of the scrolls, and the similarity of the writers' beliefs and practices to early Christianity, are subject to much less debate.

Small Group Bible Discovery and Discussion (19 minutes)

Living in the Light

The Essenes formed in response to Hellenism, the secular worldview that glorified the human being and emphasized physical perfection and personal pleasure. Under the influence of Hellenism, many religious Jews abandoned their biblical worldview. The Essenes, however, deliberately chose to remove themselves from Hellenistic culture and create communities in which they could worship and honor Yahweh. They believed there was a great struggle between the sons of light (God's followers) and the sons of darkness (Satan's followers), and they were determined to be on God's side of the struggle. Their passionate commitment exerted profound influence on the theological climate of their culture.

1.   The Essenes were keenly aware of the significance of the struggle between light and darkness. It was an important theme in the teachings of Jesus as well.

   a.   What do we learn from John 3:16 – 21 and 12:35 – 36 about the conflict between good (light) and evil (darkness)?

   b.   What was Jesus' challenge to his disciples right after he taught the Beatitudes? (See Matthew 5:14 – 16.)

2.   If we have chosen to walk with God, why is it so important to "walk in the light"? (See Ephesians 5:8 – 17; Romans 13:12 – 14; 1 John 1:5 – 7.)

What does the phrase "walk in the light" mean, and how do we go about doing it?

3. Why can't spiritual light and spiritual darkness coexist? (See 2 Corinthians 6:14 – 7:1.)

In this admonition for holy living written by the apostle Paul, what similarities do you see to the Essenes' theology and life-style?

Faith Lesson (6 minutes)

The Bible emphasizes the need for God's people to be holy, to have fellowship with God, and to walk in his light rather than in darkness. First Peter 2:9 explains the nature of our holy calling: "But you are a chosen people, a royal priesthood, a holy nation, a people belonging to God, that you may declare the praises of him who called you out of darkness into his wonderful light."

1. What does "being in his wonderful light" mean to you?

Which challenges do you face as you seek to live in his light and not in the darkness?

What challenges do you face as you seek to live in the light and at the same time live among people who live in darkness?

2. In what ways does the "light" and "darkness" imagery used in the Bible still communicate well in today's culture?

Which modern-day values or practices might be similar to the Hellenistic values (darkness) from which the Essenes fled?

3. Today, Christians face the same challenge the Essenes faced — to turn away from spiritual darkness and live as children of the light. What personal compromise(s) do you make with the values or beliefs of darkness? If you are willing, write out your commitment to remove that spiritual darkness from your life and to "put on the armor of light" in every area of your life.

Closing (1 minute)

Read aloud Luke 11:35 – 36: "See to it, then, that the light within you is not darkness. Therefore, if your whole body is full of light, and no part of it dark, it will be completely lighted, as when the light of a lamp shines on you." Then pray together, asking God to help you put aside whatever spiritual darkness exists in your heart and life so that you may shine as a light for him. Thank him for the shed blood of Jesus Christ that releases us from spiritual darkness. Commit yourself to seek his holiness, confront evil, and exhibit God's light to a watching, hurting world.

Memorize

See to it, then, that the light within you is not darkness. Therefore, if your whole body is full of light, and no part of it dark, it will be completely lighted, as when the light of a lamp shines on you.

Luke 11:35 – 36

Understanding the World in Which Jesus Lived

In-Depth Personal Study Sessions

Day One | Lessons in the Wilderness

The Very Words of God

> *Remember how the Lord your God led you all the way in the desert these forty years, to humble you and to test you in order to know what was in your heart, whether or not you would keep his commands. He humbled you, causing you to hunger and then feeding you with manna, which neither you nor your fathers had known, to teach you that man does not live on bread alone but on every word that comes from the mouth of the Lord.*
>
> Deuteronomy 8:2 – 3

Bible Discovery

The Wilderness: Preparation for an Assignment from God

The "vast and dreadful desert" wilderness (Deuteronomy 8:15) had a profound effect on God's chosen people. There, God formed them into his own people. He disciplined them for their lack of faith, disobedience, and complaining. He taught them how to serve him. He transformed them from a group of oppressed refugees into a powerful nation called to live in obedience to God in the Promised Land.

1. The Essenes knew that Israel's forefathers had spent time in the desert. What was it about the desert experiences of Israel's forefathers that helped prepare them for the missions God gave them? (See Genesis 12:1 – 9; Exodus 2:15 – 22; 3:1; 1 Samuel 23:19 – 25; 24:1 – 2.)

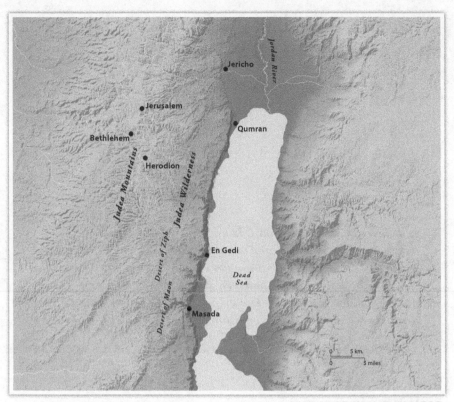

THE JUDEA WILDERNESS

2. After God delivered the Israelites from Egypt and provided
    their food and water for three months as they traversed the
    deserts, what did he do? (See Exodus 19:1 – 6; 20:1 – 17.)

Why do you think he chose that time and place?

DID YOU KNOW?
Lessons of the Wilderness

The Hebrews' forty-year wilderness journey made such an impact on them that later biblical writers and prophets referred to those days as reminders of essential truths:

- The psalmist reminded Israel of God's faithful love that was demonstrated to them in the wilderness (Psalm 105:38–45; 107:4–9).
- Jeremiah (Jeremiah 2:6; 7:22–24) and Micah (Micah 6:3–5) reminded the people of the lessons they learned in the wilderness.
- New Testament writers compared the Israelites' wilderness experience to the lives of believers (Hebrews 3:12–19; 1 Corinthians 10:1–13).
- Jesus, the new "Adam," faced Satan on our behalf in the Judea Wilderness and used lessons from the wilderness to defeat him: "Man does not live on bread alone" (Matthew 4:4; see also Deuteronomy 8:3); and "Do not put the Lord your God to the test" (Matthew 4:7; see also Deuteronomy 6:16).

3. What do the following passages reveal about how God prepared the Israelites in the wilderness? (See Deuteronomy 8:1 - 5, 10 - 18; Psalm 95:6 - 11; Jeremiah 2:1 - 3.)

How might the Essenes have been seeking to duplicate similar experiences in their desert community so that they would be better prepared to serve God and fulfill their calling in the world?

4. When the Israelites turned from God, what did he want them to remember? Why do you think God did this? (See Psalm 81:6 – 16; Jeremiah 2:4 – 8; 31:31 – 32.)

DID YOU KNOW?

The landscape of Israel played a significant role in biblical history and imagery. Much of Israel's terrain is rugged desert, referred to as "wilderness" in the Scriptures. These wilderness areas were close to where most Israelites lived.

The *Negev Wilderness* was barely forty miles south of Jerusalem. This arid land can be divided into three distinct regions. The northern region, with its rolling hills and broad valleys, is good sheep country. The central region, including the Zin Wilderness, has rugged, deep canyons and is inhospitable even to nomads. The southern region, called the Wilderness of Paran, is the most barren of all.

The *Judea Wilderness* began just east of Jerusalem and was within sight of anyone who lived in the central mountains. This wilderness borders the fertile mountain ridge to the west for more than fifty miles, forming a distinct line between farmland and wilderness.

Because the wilderness, particularly the Judea Wilderness, was so close to settled areas, it became a refuge for those seeking solitude or safety from authorities. In the wilderness David hid from Saul (1 Samuel 26), John the Baptist isolated himself from the usual religious practices of the day (Matthew 3), and Jesus faced the devil (Matthew 4). The wilderness was also where the Essenes labored over their scrolls and early Christians built monasteries, some of which still function today.

Reflection

Although many of us do our best to avoid "wilderness" experiences, there is much that God would have us learn there — not only from our own times in the wilderness but from the desert experiences of the ancient Israelites. Notice what the apostle Paul, a respected rabbi who was well-versed in the Hebrew Scriptures, taught the Corinthians about the Israelites' wilderness experience:

> *For I do not want you to be ignorant of the fact, brothers, that our forefathers were all under the cloud and that they all passed through the sea. They were all baptized into Moses in the cloud and in the sea. They all ate the same spiritual food and drank the same spiritual drink; for they drank from the spiritual rock that accompanied them, and that rock was Christ. Nevertheless, God was not pleased with most of them; their bodies were scattered over the desert.*
>
> *Now these things occurred as examples to keep us from setting our hearts on evil things as they did. Do not be idolaters, as some of them were; as it is written: "The people sat down to eat and drink and got up to indulge in pagan revelry." We should not commit sexual immorality, as some of them did — and in one day twenty-three thousand of them died. We should not test the Lord, as some of them did — and were killed by snakes. And do not grumble, as some of them did — and were killed by the destroying angel.*
>
> *These things happened to them as examples and were written down as warnings for us, on whom the fulfillment of the ages has come. So, if you think you are standing firm, be careful that you don't fall!*
>
> *1 Corinthians 10:1 – 12*

What can we gain by studying what happened to the ancient Israelites in the wilderness?

Why is it important for us to not only know but to apply the lessons of their experiences to our lives?

In Paul's letter, he relates the Israelites' struggle against sin to the experiences of Christians in his day.

Which particular sin(s) of the Israelites do you see prominently evidenced in your culture, and how much are these sins a part of your life?

Which "evil things" have you set your heart on that are causing you to fall?

What is your commitment to confess and repent from these sins in order to walk with God?

If you were to summarize what you have learned during your own "wilderness" experiences, how is it similar to what God taught the ancient Israelites in the wilderness? How valuable to you are these experiences?

Memorize

I will remember the deeds of the LORD; yes, I will remember your miracles of long ago. I will meditate on all your works and consider all your mighty deeds.

Psalm 77:11 – 12

Day Two | God Brings Redemption through the Wilderness

The Very Words of God

> *Praise be to the Lord, the God of Israel, because he has come and has redeemed his people. He has raised up a horn of salvation for us in the house of his servant David (as he said through his holy prophets of long ago).*

> Luke 1:68–70

Bible Discovery

The Wilderness Is a Tool in God's Hands

Many times God accomplished his redemptive work through the challenges of the wilderness. In the wilderness, God's people faced hardship and temptation. Through the difficulties of their wilderness circumstances, God got their full attention. They learned to focus on what God wanted to accomplish and to look to him for everything they needed.

1. What role did the prophet Hosea say the wilderness would play in restoring God's unfaithful bride, Israel, to her rightful place with him? (See Hosea 2:14–23.)

2. For what purposes did John the Baptist go into the wilderness? (See Matthew 3:1–6.)

3. Matthew 3:13 – 4:11 reveals that as soon as Jesus came up out of the Jordan River following his baptism, he was led into the desert — the same wilderness in which the Essene community of Qumran was located — to be tempted by Satan.

   a. Why was the wilderness an appropriate setting for Jesus' temptation? (See Isaiah 40:1 – 5.)

   b. How did Jesus resist Satan's forty-day spiritual attack? (See Luke 4:1 – 13.)

   c. Why did Jesus have to be tempted? What is the importance of his resistance to Satan compared with Adam's lack of resistance? (See Romans 5:12 – 19.)

   d. What do 1 Corinthians 10:13 and Hebrews 2:14 – 18 reveal about the importance of Jesus' temptation in the wilderness?

Reflection

Just as the desert wilderness played a role in God's plan of redemption long ago, believers today also face times in the wilderness (although not usually the desert). We face difficult times when we may be tempted to doubt God and his Word. We face uncertainty and fear, and may even wonder how God could possibly be preparing us to accomplish his redemptive purposes.

What kind of courage do you think it took for Jesus to go into the wilderness alone, fast for an extended time, and face the evil one?

As a result of the way in which Jesus was tempted in the wilderness, what have you learned about temptation and the importance of accomplishing God's work according to his plan?

Does a follower of Jesus ever face the evil one alone? Why or why not?

Why, during your spiritual journey, must you know and rely on the Word of God in order to stand against temptation and sin?

How can you know that, whatever your life is like right now, God still desires to use you in a special way to further his kingdom?

Day Three | A Community Set Apart to Fulfill God's Plan

The Very Words of God

> *As the rain and the snow come down from heaven, and do not return to it without watering the earth and making it bud and flourish, so that it yields seed for the sower and bread for the eater, so is my word that goes out from my mouth: It will not return to me empty, but will accomplish what I desire and achieve the purpose for which I sent it.*
>
> Isaiah 55:10 – 11

Bible Discovery

A Commitment to Live for God Bears Fruit

For centuries God worked through people to prepare the world for the advent of his Son, the Messiah. He chose his people, Israel; preserved the line of David; brought his people back from exile to the Promised Land. He even set apart a wilderness community of devout Jews at Qumran to provide the cultural and theological context for Jesus' life and work. So when Jesus came, his message fell on fertile soil — prepared in part by the Essenes who dedicated themselves to the pure worship of Yahweh and waited expectantly for the Messiah.

1. The Essene lifestyle included teachings and practices that were similar to those of Jesus and the early Christians, which helped to enhance the popular acceptance of Jesus' message. Even today, the impact of their lifestyle and beliefs provides insight into how God uses people to unfold his plan of redemption. Consider how the lifestyle of the Essene community helped to prepare the first-century world to receive the Messiah.

a. As a community, the Essenes held their personal possessions in common. In what ways was this similar to the
lifestyle of the early Christians? (See Acts 2:42 – 45.)

b. The Essenes practiced a ceremonial meal that symbolized a great messianic banquet they believed would
occur when the Messiah arrived. During this meal, they
blessed bread and wine. What symbolic meal did Jesus
establish that Christians still keep today? (See Matthew
26:26 – 29.)

c. The Essenes practiced a ceremonial cleansing using living, free-flowing water that symbolized the spiritual
cleansing of repentance and forgiveness. What type of
symbolic cleansing did the early Christians practice? (See
John 3:22 – 23; Acts 2:36 – 41.)

2. What do Galatians 4:4 – 5 and Romans 8:28 reveal about the
timing of God's redemptive plan?

What does this tell you about the role of the Essenes in preparing the way for Jesus?

What does this reveal about God's timing in the lives of all of his followers — including you?

Reflection

Through the Essenes, we see yet another way in which God set apart specific people — in this case a community of committed Jews — to pave the way for the living Word, Jesus Christ the Messiah, who was coming to redeem the world.

As you think about how the Essenes set themselves apart to live for God, and realize how similar their lifestyle was to that of the early Christians, how does their lifestyle influence your commitment to live for God?

How important is it, for example, for you to study faithfully God's Word, which for centuries he has preserved and protected?

How important is repentance, forgiveness, and pure living in your everyday life?

What does God's careful preparation for Jesus' coming say to you about his character and the relationship he desires to have with you?

In what way(s) have you seen evidence of God's careful planning in your life?

If you are a follower of Jesus, you have a part in God's ongoing redemptive plan. How great is your desire to live in such a way that God's purpose will be fulfilled in you for the redemption of people around you and for future generations?

Memorize

*The plans of the L*ORD *stand firm forever, the purposes of his heart through all generations.*

Psalm 33:11

COMPELLING EVIDENCE
The Remains of Qumran

As is true with many ancient settlements, Qumran was destroyed and rebuilt various times. The earliest settlement on the site dates to the Israelite period shortly before the Babylonian Captivity (c. 600 BC), when it was probably destroyed. Around 140 BC, Qumran was resettled during the reign of the Hasmonaean king Hyrcanus, but the settlement was abandoned after a damaging earthquake (c. 31 BC). Resettled about the time Jesus was born, Qumran became an active community until the Roman army, under Vespasian's command, destroyed it in approximately AD 68.

The major structures in Qumran provide significant evidence of the community's lifestyle and beliefs:

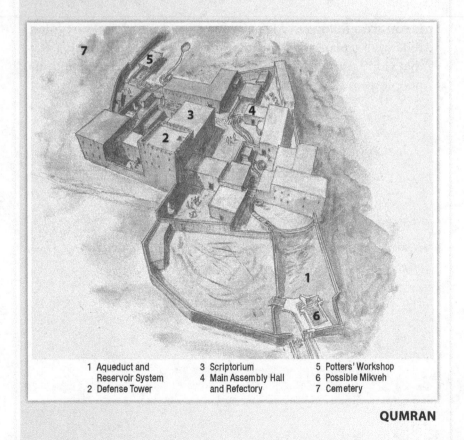

1 Aqueduct and Reservoir System	3 Scriptorium	5 Potters' Workshop
2 Defense Tower	4 Main Assembly Hall and Refectory	6 Possible Mikveh
		7 Cemetery

QUMRAN

Aqueduct and Reservoir System

The Essenes' commitment to doing what they believed God wanted them to do is exemplary. They believed that water used as a symbol of purification must be "living" or moving, not drawn by hand, so they developed a system in which rainwater ran on its own into a ritual bath. In the steep, rocky wadi just west of their community, they created catch basins where runoff from the Judea Wilderness cascaded over a cliff. They tunneled more than 100 feet through solid rock to bring that water to the cliff's edge, then directed the water through more than a thousand feet of plaster-coated channels and aqueducts until it reached the community, where it was stored in cisterns.

At least two cisterns were probably used as ceremonial or ritual baths (*mikvoth)* and had steps that allowed access to the water. New members were cleansed with water in a type of baptism that apparently symbolized the spiritual cleansing that resulted from repentance and forgiveness after any breaking of God's laws. (See Matthew 3:6, 11.) The Essenes' ritual cleansing likely provided

AN ESSENE CISTERN

the background for the baptism practiced by John the Baptist and for the baptism practiced by the early Christians.

Defense Tower

Scholars debate the importance of the large tower that once stood in Qumran because essentially its community of religious separatists lived a peaceful, almost monastic existence. The Essenes did, however, believe in the Messiah's imminent arrival and that a great battle would ensue between the sons of light (themselves) and the sons of darkness (followers of evil). The

continued on next page . . .

tower most likely provided protection against bandits or other less "military" threats.

Scriptorium

Archaeologists believe that the Dead Sea Scrolls were written in this area. Excavation has revealed tables and benches similar to those used by scribes, as well as inkpots and basins in which the Essenes could ritualistically wash their hands before and after writing God's sacred name.

Main Assembly Hall and Refectory

In this room, archaeologists believe the Essenes practiced a communal meal in anticipation of the great banquet of the messianic age. Scholars have discovered many similarities between the Essenes' ceremonial meal and the Last Supper recorded in the Gospels (Matthew 26:26–29).

In one corner of the room, a small water channel entered where the floor sloped down toward the opposite end of the room. This may have allowed the room to be washed in preparation for the meal. Nearby, archaeologists have unearthed a kitchen with five fireplaces and a smaller room containing the remains of more than a thousand pottery jars, dishes, plates, and cups. Interestingly, community members did not live in this or any other buildings uncovered by archaeologists. They may have lived in nearby caves or tents.

QUMRAN: THE MAIN ASSEMBLY HALL

Potters' Workshop

Here, archaeologists have found a basin for preparing clay, a base for a potter's wheel, and two kilns. The clay jars, which helped to preserve the Dead Sea Scrolls for nearly 2,000 years, were probably made here.

Cemetery

The main cemetery east of Qumran contains more than a thousand carefully arranged grave sites in orderly rows. Each grave was marked by a small mound of stones, and individuals were buried with their heads facing south. Although ancient writers, including Josephus, indicated that no women lived among the Essenes, women are buried in several of the graves. Scholars have suggested that these were family members of the Qumran community.

Day Four | Preparing Hearts and Minds to Receive the Messiah

The Very Words of God

> *The people walking in darkness have seen a great light; on those living in the land of the shadow of death a light has dawned.*

Isaiah 9:2

Bible Discovery

The Essenes Develop New Theological Concepts and Terminology

As they devoted themselves to God and the study of the Hebrew Scriptures, the Essenes not only developed a lifestyle that would in some ways be similar to that of the early Christians, they developed theological concepts and terminology that are similar, or even identical, to those expressed by the New Testament writers. Consider how the Essenes' understanding of theology contributed to the ability of first century people to accept Jesus as the Messiah.

1. In the Dead Sea Scrolls, the Essenes used each of the following words or phrases, which are common to the New Testament

but not elsewhere, long before Jesus was born. Match the words and phrases below to the following New Testament Scriptures: Matthew 3:3; 5:3; 6:22 – 23; Luke 1:32, 35; John 1:5; 3:19 – 21; 12:36; 2 Corinthians 6:14 – 15; Hebrews 7:1 – 3.

Words or Phrases Used by the Essenes	New Testament Reference
sons of light	
light and darkness	
Belial	
poor in spirit	
Melchizedek	
Son of God (Son of the Most High)	
way of the Lord	

How would the Essenes' use of the terminology above have prepared Jesus' audience to better understand his teachings and message?

2. The Essenes interpreted prophetic Scriptures as being fulfilled by the events of their day, which differed significantly from other religious movements of their time. Why was acceptance, or at least knowledge, of this concept important to God's plan of redemption? (See Matthew 3:1 – 3; Luke 4:14 – 21, 18:31 – 33; Acts 2:14 – 36.)

WORTH OBSERVING
God's Perfect Timing

Scripture reveals that God arranged many significant events, movements, and people in order to make the timing of Jesus' birth perfect for the beginning of the church. According to Galatians 4:4–5, "when the time had fully come, God sent his Son, born of a woman, … to redeem." Timing-related factors include:

- The conquests of Alexander the Great, 350 years before Jesus, which made the known world conversant in one language—Greek. This significantly increased the early spread of the gospel.
- World dominion by the Roman Empire, which provided world peace and a wide network of roads built for the Roman legions and trade that Christian missionaries later used. The Romans also executed by crucifixion, and the psalmist had predicted that Jesus would be pierced at his execution (Psalm 22:16–17).

3. The Essenes traced the priesthood of the Messiah to Melchizedek, not Aaron. Why is this belief essential to accepting Jesus as the Messiah? (See Luke 1:31 – 33; Hebrews 7:1 - 22.)

4. Even though the Essenes had many beliefs in common with the early Christians, there were key differences between them. For example, compare:

   a. The Essenes' belief in two messiahs (a priest and a king) with Hebrews 7:15 - 17; 8:1 - 2; Luke 1:32 - 33.

b. The Essenes' practice of living separately from the world
    with Matthew 28:19 – 20.

c. The Essenes' strict Sabbath observance with Matthew
    12:1 – 13.

Reflection

God's work in history is rarely sudden and dramatic. Rather, he
works through the process of history and the lives of people. Just
as he used the Romans and the Essenes to prepare a culture and
a setting in which the life, death, and resurrection of Jesus could
be understood and received, God continues to use people to bring
about his redemptive plans. He wants to use you as well!

In what ways might God already be using you — among family
members, at the office, at school, in your neighborhood?

In light of the fact that God is always unfolding his plans
through us individually and through the course of history, how
important is it for you to renew your determination to make
choices that will honor him?

What specific things are you doing that will cause the light
of God to dawn on those who are living in darkness?

How might you put your skills, resources, gifts, and abilities to better use as you partner with God to share the light of his coming with people you know?

WAS JOHN THE BAPTIST AN ESSENE?

Did John the Baptist live at Qumran? See the Dead Sea Scrolls? Write any of them? These questions have gripped scholars because the scrolls reveal remarkable similarities between the Essenes and John's teaching and practices. However, John was never identified as an Essene. He was not a member of any community and can't be placed definitively at Qumran. Furthermore, he proclaimed his message publicly rather than seeking the isolation of a monastic setting. Note the following comparisons:

John the Baptist	The Essenes
Came from family of priests (Luke 1:5)	Many were priests who disagreed with temple authorities
Lived in the wilderness (Luke 1:80)	Qumran was in the Judea Wilderness
Was called to "prepare the way for the Lord" (Isaiah 40:1–5)	Lived in the wilderness to prepare the way for the Lord
Baptized as a sign of repentance and inner cleansing (Mark 1:4–5)	Practiced ritual cleansing in water as a sign of the soul's cleansing
Proclaimed that the One to come would baptize with the Holy Spirit (Mark 1:7–8)	Believed God would pour out his Spirit like water to cleanse perverse hearts
Was not accepted by most people (Matthew 21:32)	Complained that people ignored their teachings
Didn't participate in the normal lifestyle of his people (Mark 1:6)	Lived an ascetic existence; prepared their own food
His disciples fasted and recited prayers (Mark 2:18; Luke 11:1)	Fasted; had specific prayers
Was in conflict with Jerusalem authorities (Matthew 3:7–10)	Wanted to create a new temple and religious practices

Day Five | Called to Evangelize, Not to Separate

The Very Words of God

> *Later Jesus appeared to the Eleven as they were eating; he rebuked them for their lack of faith and their stubborn refusal to believe those who had seen him after he had risen. He said to them, "Go into all the world and preach the good news to all creation."*
>
> **Mark 16:14 – 15**

Bible Discovery

Called to Go into the World

God used the Essenes, who separated themselves from the prevailing culture in order to know and worship God, to help prepare the way for the coming of Jesus. The Essenes' devotion led to new ways to honor God with one's life and brought to light theological concepts that provided a context in which Jews of the first century could better understand the message of Jesus. But once Jesus accomplished his work of redemption, the challenge for his followers was not so much to separate *from* the world, but to take the good news of redemption *into* the world.

1. What did Jesus command his disciples to do so that they might continue to advance God's plan of redemption? (See Matthew 28:19 – 20.)

2. In Matthew 5:13 – 16, what images did Jesus use to illustrate the role his disciples were to have in the world? How actively were they to do this?

How do we know that Jesus' disciples did this? (See Romans 1:8; Colossians 1:3 – 6; 1 Thessalonians 1:6 – 8.)

3. Above all else, which redemptive characteristic were early Christians to model as they shared the gospel message in many nations? (See Mark 12:30 – 31; Luke 6:32 – 35; John 13:34 – 35.)

Reflection

Without compromising our calling to walk as Jesus walked, Christians are to interact with people who live in spiritual darkness and, by the power of God, to confront evil. We are, as God's ambassadors, to shed his light in a dark and watching world.

If you and Jesus were to have breakfast or meet for coffee tomorrow, what would he say about your willingness to share his message of redemption with people who don't know him — at work, in your neighborhood, at school, wherever?

The Essenes' commitment to live completely for God led to their having a role in preparing the way for the Messiah. As Christians, we need to live a life in the world that is fully committed to God so that we can fulfill our role in God's plan.

So, how dedicated are you to knowing, studying, and living by God's Word?

How much effort will you put into obeying him in every-thing?

How often do you talk with God about your love for him, your desire to serve him, and your need for his strength and guidance as you seek to fulfill his calling?

Which sins are hindering your ability to reflect the light of Jesus in your everyday world? Will you confess them and turn away from them?

Which specific thing(s) will you do to share — by word and by action — the truth of God's gift of redemption with at least one person this week?

Memorize

Therefore go and make disciples of all nations, baptizing them in the name of the Father and of the Son and of the Holy Spirit, and teaching them to obey everything I have commanded you. And surely I am with you always, to the very end of the age.

Matthew 28:19–20

DATA FILE
A Brief History of the Essenes

In 332 BC, Alexander the Great's armies swept through Israel, and his successors continued his campaign to bring Greek culture to every part of the known world. The Hellenistic culture deeply offended and disturbed devout Jews, but most Jewish people were soon seduced by this secular worldview that glorified the human being through philosophy, athletics, religion, and the arts.

Initially, Alexander's successors — the Ptolemy family from Egypt — allowed significant religious freedom for the Jews. During their rule, the Old Testament was translated into Greek, the translation we know as the Septuagint. Later, the Seleucids — Syria's Greek dynasty — brought Israel into their empire. They aggressively promoted Greek culture, defiled the temple in Jerusalem with pigs' blood, and dedicated it to their god, Zeus. They banned the Torah, the Sabbath observance, and circumcision. To violate these bans meant death.

Faithful Jews, led by the Hasmonaean family (also known as the Maccabees) revolted and drove out the pagans. For the first time in nearly 500 years, the Jews were independent. The temple was cleansed and rededicated, and worship of Yahweh resumed. Their great victory became the focus of the Feast of Dedication, known today as Hanukkah (John 10:22).

The Hasmonaean descendants, however, became thoroughly Hellenistic. They openly flaunted pagan practices and fought bitterly with followers of the Torah. When Jonathan the Hasmonaean, who was a Hellenist and not from the line of Zadok (as required by pious Jews), assumed the office of high priest, that was the final straw. The Hasidim, a pious group that had strongly supported the Maccabee revolt, openly opposed the descendants of Judah.

Out of the Hasidim came two movements that greatly influenced events of the New Testament: the Pharisees and the Essenes. Scholars believe that when Jonathan was appointed, the Essenes established a religious movement dedicated to the restoration of the true worship of God. Believing them-

continued on next page . . .

selves to be the sons of light preparing for a great battle with the sons of darkness, the Essenes felt they needed to be ready to take their place in God's army. Their mission was to prepare the way for the Lord. So, they sought to keep their hearts and minds pure and their practices obedient.

Stricter than Pharisees in observing the Sabbath, the Essenes established many practices that set the stage for Jesus' arrival and teaching. They practiced ritual washing to purify themselves of sin, spent much time studying and carefully copying sacred texts, and practiced obedience to God and justice to mankind. Although small in number, they exerted significant influence on the religious community of their day.

In 68 AD, the Romans destroyed the Essene community at Qumran. It is possible that the Essenes placed their sacred scrolls in jars and hid them in nearby caves as the Romans approached. Although this community has disappeared from history, its legacy is only now being realized.

NO GREATER LOVE

The beautiful hillside overlooking the Sea of Galilee known as the "Mount of Beatitudes" and the ruins of Korazin just a few miles to the north provide insights into the cultural background of Galilee at the time of Jesus. This glimpse into the world in which Jesus lived can help us better understand his teaching about heaven and our eternal relationship with him.

As Jesus taught, for example, he compared himself to a bridegroom who was engaged to be married: "I love you as my bride," he said, in effect, "so I'll pay the bride price. I'll give up my life for you. I'll go to my Father's house where there are many rooms and prepare a place for you. One day I will return and take you to be with me forever in heaven." To understand the full meaning of Jesus' love for us, it is helpful to know something about the lifestyle and marriage customs of Jewish families at that time.

When it was time for a man and woman to marry, both fathers would negotiate the bride price that would compensate the family of the bride-to-be. After exchanging a glass of wine to seal the agreement, the couple was formally engaged. Then the young man would say to his fiancée, in effect, "I'm going home to my father's house to prepare a place for you. When I've done that, I'll return and take you to be my wife."

The husband-to-be (typically in his mid-twenties) then built a new house onto his father's existing one. As generations married and continued this practice, they created a housing complex called an *insula*. Here, family members ate, worked, and lived together.

Children knew their grandparents, aunts, uncles, cousins, nieces, and nephews. Everyone benefited as family members shared their lives and values.

As her fiancé and his father prepared her new home, the bride-to-be (typically fourteen or fifteen years old) remained with her parents, preparing wedding clothes and learning homemaking skills. During this time, she was known as "one who had been bought with a price." She might wait six or nine months, or even longer, for her beloved. No one knew the exact time when he would come for her.

After completing the house, the husband-to-be would gather his friends and family and go to his fiancée's house to announce the wedding and take his bride home. People would gather in the open courtyard of the *insula*, and the "best man" would stand by the door of the wedding chamber while the couple consummated the marriage. Then he would announce that the wedding had taken place, and a joyous, seven-day reception followed.

By using the familiar metaphors of wedding customs and the *insula*, Jesus was making a powerful statement about his love for and commitment to those who have accepted him as Lord and Savior. Life in heaven will be like a joyous wedding reception, celebrating the love between the bride and Bridegroom. Everyone will live together as one family. This metaphor also helps us understand Jesus' important teaching about love, community, and support. Only by living in this way could the people of Jesus' day (and ours) be the vibrant, caring, influential community Jesus founded in his bride — the church.

Not only was Jesus' message about the kingdom of heaven important, but the location of much of his ministry was also significant. He conducted most of his healing and teaching ministry in the vicinity of the Sea of Galilee, specifically the small "gospel triangle" of Bethsaida, Korazin, and Capernaum. By teaching in this region, Jesus fulfilled Isaiah's words: "In the future he will honor Galilee of the Gentiles, by the way of the sea, along the Jordan — The people walking in darkness have seen a great light; on those living in the land of the shadow of death a light has dawned" (Isaiah 9:1 – 2).

In addition, Capernaum was a toll stop on the Via Maris, the trade route of the ancient world. By teaching in Galilee, Jesus interacted with devout Jews, pagans, Zealots, powerbrokers of the Jewish community, farmers, and merchants. Because Galilee was a crossroads of the ancient world, Jesus' message about the kingdom of heaven spread throughout the world.

Opening Thoughts (4 minutes)

The Very Words of God

> You are not your own; you were bought at a price.
>
> *1 Corinthians 6:19 – 20*

Think About It

During his time on earth, Jesus often described his kingdom in terms of common cultural experiences that his audience would readily understand.

Which experiences are common to many people in our culture today, and how might you use them to explain the gospel message to another person?

DVD Teaching Notes (22 minutes)

The Sermon on the Mount: God's battle plan

Korazin, a typical Galilean city

Jewish marriage customs

Jesus will come for his bride

DVD Discussion (7 minutes)

1. Look at the map of Galilee on page 121, and note the cities and towns of the region in which this video was filmed. Which cities are closest to the Via Maris? What were the characteristics of the cities and regions surrounding the Sea of Galilee?

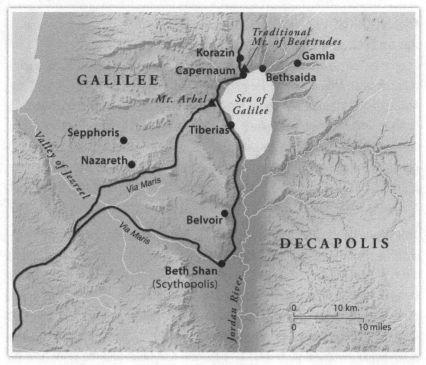

GALILEE

2. What did you learn about Jewish community life and the
    marriage customs in first-century Galilee that enhanced your
    understanding of God's love for you?

3. Why is the message of the Beatitudes so important to Chris-
    tians today?

DID YOU KNOW?
Jesus Probably Lived with His Extended Family

People in Galilee often lived in family housing complexes called *insulae* (singular *insula*). Although not everyone lived this way, many people — particularly extended families — combined living units around an open courtyard. In such a family community, values could be passed on to the next generation as children lived and worked with parents, grandparents, uncles, aunts, and cousins. The strength of the extended family's values also provided incentive for individual members to live obediently before God in order to not dishonor the household.

The *insula* is also the basis for the New Testament references to "household," which means "an extended family living together." Jesus referred to various households in his teaching (Matthew 10:24–25, 36). After Jesus healed the official's son, "he and all his household believed" (John 4:53). Peter described how an angel had appeared to a Gentile man and said that he (Peter) would bring a message through which the man and *all his household* would be saved (Acts 11:11–14). Paul and Silas told the jailer how he and *all his household* could be saved (Acts 16:29–32).

AN INSULA

Although we can't know for sure, it is possible that Jesus and his disciples lived in an *insula* in Capernaum (Matthew 12:46–13:1, 36; Mark 2:1–2; 7:17). The image of an extended family household that an *insula* provides fits with the New Testament understanding of how Jesus' followers would relate as a community. The *insula*, for example, is the basis for one of the pictures of heaven (God's housing complex) mentioned in John 14:2. God also considers the church to be God's household (Ephesians 2:19; 1 Timothy 3:15).

Small Group Bible Discovery and Discussion (16 minutes)

Jesus' Relationship with His Bride — the Church

Jesus often used the metaphor of the marriage relationship to describe his love for his disciples. It was a familiar and deeply meaningful image for Jewish people of Jesus' day. To better understand this beautiful, poignant imagery, let's consider how certain Jewish cultural practices help to convey New Testament teaching.

1. When a young man wanted to marry, his family agreed to pay a bride price (usually a large sum) to compensate the bride's family for the loss of their daughter. What price did Jesus pay for you? (See 1 Corinthians 6:19–20; Galatians 3:13–14; 1 Peter 1:18–19.)

   What does the price Jesus was willing to pay for his "bride" say about the depth of his love?

2. In first-century Israel, an engagement was as serious as mar-
    riage. (Breaking an engagement required a divorce.) After
    the families agreed on the "bride price," the couple drank
    a glass of wine together to seal their commitment to each
    other. How does your knowledge of this engagement custom
    enhance your understanding of Matthew 26:27 – 28, Mark
    14:23 – 25, and Luke 22:20?

3. After his betrothal, the husband-to-be returned to his father's
    household and, supervised by his father, prepared a place for
    his bride by adding on to the family *insula*. Where is Jesus,
    our Bridegroom, and what is he doing? (See John 14:1 – 3.)

**BUILDING A TYPICAL
GALILEAN HOME**

What, then, is our destination, and what should we be preparing to do?

How should we live if we are spiritually "engaged" to Jesus?

What specifically do you think we should do to prepare for our future life with him?

Faith Lesson (5 minutes)

Set in the context of first-century Jewish marriage customs, Jesus' words in John 14:1 – 3 offer an amazing promise and invitation to all believers.

1. Jesus gave the ultimate sacrifice — his life — to purchase salvation for each of us. As Christians, we each belong to the church Jesus founded and as such are the "bride" of Jesus. If you are a Christian, what does it mean to you that Jesus presents himself as your spiritual "husband"?

   What difference does it make to your everyday life that Jesus has bought you with a price — just as a husband-to-be bought his beloved bride — and is eagerly preparing an eternal home for you?

2. What have you discovered during this session about the depth of Jesus' love for you?

In what ways has his love for you as his "bride" become more meaningful to you?

To what extent have you realized that Jesus is eager to have fellowship with you and be with you — much like a young man who wants to be with his beloved?

If you have a hard time recognizing or accepting Jesus' love for you, how might you become more open to receiving his love?

Closing (1 minute)

Read John 14:1 – 3 aloud: "Do not let your hearts be troubled. Trust in God; trust also in me. In my Father's house are many rooms; if it were not so, I would have told you. I am going there to prepare a place for you. And if I go and prepare a place for you, I will come back and take you to be with me that you also may be where I am." Then pray, asking God to let his love permeate your hearts and minds. The God of the universe has promised to every believer life with him in heaven. He invites us to respond to his love and trust in him!

Memorize

Do not let your hearts be troubled. Trust in God; trust also in me. In my Father's house are many rooms; if it were not so, I would have told you. I am going there to prepare a place for you. And if I go and prepare a place for you, I will come back and take you to be with me that you also may be where I am.

John 14:1 – 3

DATA FILE
Inside a First-Century Jewish House

In Galilee, the ancient village of Qatzrin has been excavated and recon-structed. Although it was populated centuries after Jesus' time, scholars believe that the buildings and artifacts discovered there represent the liv-ing conditions of first-century Galileans. Houses in Korazin, Bethsaida, and Capernaum (where Jesus lived, healed, and taught) were built in the same style using similar materials. By learning more about the homes and lives of everyday people during biblical times, we can better picture the way Jesus lived.

A typical Galilean home was built of basalt (dark volcanic rock) and had either one or two stories. A stonemason (sometimes translated as a "carpen-ter") used a wooden scaffold as he carefully squared the larger rocks and wedged smaller stones in-between to provide stability and strength. Some-times walls were plastered with mud and straw. The doorframe was built of shaped stones and covered by a wooden door. A courtyard, located between various rooms of a family's housing complex, was paved with stones.

Roofs often were made of wooden beams topped with tree branches and covered with clay. When it rained, the clay absorbed water, sealing the roof. (In Korazin, however, roofs were made of stone slabs instead of branches.) Sometimes people did their work and slept on their roofs (Matthew 24:17; Mark 13:15; Acts 10:9), which needed to be repaired every year.

continued on next page . . .

A typical Galilean kitchen contained a domed oven for cooking and heating when the weather was cold. Animal dung, the pulp of pressed olives, and small branches were used as fuel. Common kitchen utensils included hand grinders for making flour, cooking pots, reed or palm-leaf baskets for gathering and storing food, a broom, and stone water jars. Small gardens, vineyards, olive trees, and some small livestock provided most of the people's food.

A GALILEAN KITCHEN

A Galilean family room, the center of family life, was probably used for eating, storing food, and socializing when the weather was inappropriate for being outdoors in the courtyard. Wealthy people reclined as they ate; poorer people sat on the floor or on benches. Food was served on pottery plates or in pottery bowls. Jewish laws regarding "clean" and "unclean" (Matthew 23:25–26) apparently required that different pottery be used for different types of food so that meat and dairy did not mix, for example.

A GALILEAN FAMILY ROOM

PROVISIONS   THE SLEEPING LOFT

Provisions such as grain, wine, and oil were stored in large jars in cool places. (See 1 Kings 17:7 – 14; 2 Kings 4:1 – 7.) Other foods were hung from the ceiling. First-century Jews worked hard to raise their food, and it was necessary to protect it from spoilage, rodents, and insects. However, Jesus encouraged people to live by faith in God's provision and criticized those who were so obsessed with providing for their future needs that they hoarded goods (Luke 12:16 – 34).

Sleeping quarters, sometimes located on the second floor and accessed by ladder, had beds made of wooden frames with rope stretched over them. A mat then was laid on each bed. Sometimes more than one family member slept in the same bed (Luke 11:5 – 7). Poorer people often slept on mats placed on the floor. People could take their mats with them when they traveled (Matthew 9:2 – 8; Mark 2:3 – 12).

THE LAMP

Lighting was often provided by small, olive-oil lamps that were

continued on next page . . .

supplied from a goatskin oil container. Most people, however, went to bed at sunset and got up at dawn. Honest people didn't work after dark, hence the phrase "deeds of darkness" was developed (Luke 22:53; Romans 13:12; Ephesians 5:11–14).

A storeroom contained the all-important farming tools and supplies that most families needed in order to raise their own food: wooden plow, sickle, brooms, winnowing fork, a sieve for grain, rope made from plant fibers, an animal skin used as a churn for butter or cheese, etc. (The skin was hung and rocked for a long time in order to provide the churning action.) Typically a donkey or ox pulled a wooden plow with an iron point over the small fields in which grain was grown. At harvest time, farmers cut the grain with the sickle, then placed the grain on a hard stone surface called a "threshing floor" where it was crushed (threshed) by a small sled dragged by animals. Then the straw and grain mixture was thrown into the air on a windy day. The lighter straw and chaff blew away; the grain fell and was collected. Finally, the sieve separated any chaff that remained (Matthew 3:11–12; Mark 4:26–29).

THE STOREROOM

Understanding the World in Which Jesus Lived

In-Depth Personal Study Sessions

Day One | Jesus Teaches About the Kingdom of God

The Very Words of God

> *From the days of John the Baptist until now, the kingdom of heaven has been forcefully advancing, and forceful men lay hold of it. For all the Prophets and the Law prophesied until John. And if you are willing to accept it, he is the Elijah who was to come. He who has ears, let him hear.*
>
> Matthew 11:12 – 15

Bible Discovery

Battle Strategy for the Kingdom of God

As he taught his disciples and the crowds who followed him in Galilee, Jesus often talked about the kingdom of God. In fact, we could think of the Sermon on the Mount — one of Jesus' five great discourses — as Jesus' "blueprint" or battle strategy for establishing God's kingdom. It gave his followers a new covenant — a new Torah, which, if followed, would change the world.

Jesus was willing to become God's sacrifice in order to usher in God's kingdom. What he required of his followers, his *talmidim*, was no less revolutionary. In order to better understand what it means to obey Jesus' call and live as he lived, it is helpful to consider how the people of Jesus' world would have understood his teachings about kingdom living.

1. In Exodus 19:1 – 3, 20:1 – 17 we read how God gave Israel his law — the way to put into practice the values of his kingdom. Compare that event on Mount Sinai to the Sermon on the Mount, recorded in Matthew 5:1 – 12, where Jesus revealed

how he wanted his disciples to live out the values of God's kingdom.

How does Matthew 5:17 – 20 clarify the relationship between the law God gave on Mount Sinai and the "new Torah" Jesus gave on the hillside in Galilee?

2. The twelve tribes of Israel received five building blocks for kingdom living: the Old Testament books of Genesis, Exodus, Leviticus, Numbers, and Deuteronomy. Without being too detailed, briefly describe Jesus' five great discourses, which are the building blocks for his followers.

Scripture Text	How Jesus Described the Building Blocks of God's Kingdom
Matt. 5 – 7	
Matt. 10	
Matt. 13	
Matt. 18	
Matt. 24 – 25	

3. For centuries, the people of Israel had longed for the coming of the Messiah and the establishment of God's kingdom. So when Jesus, the Galilean rabbi, taught that the kingdom of God had arrived, they listened very carefully. Although they longed for the kingdom, their ideas of what it would be like and how they would participate in it differed greatly from what Jesus taught. Consider for a moment how different segments of Jesus' audience were likely to have responded to his unusual battle plan.

   a. What do you think the Zealots and the Pharisees thought when they heard Jesus speak of what is honored in his kingdom? (See Matthew 5:5, 9, 43 – 47.)

   b. How might the Sadducees and Herodians have responded to what Jesus taught in Matthew 6:19 – 24?

Reflection

Jesus' five great discourses, especially the Sermon on the Mount, remind us of what God's kingdom is all about and the vital role every Christian has in his kingdom. Just as the disciples who walked with Jesus and heard him teach in Galilee had to adjust their ideas about the kingdom of God to what Jesus taught, we need to do the same. We need to be willing to follow his revolutionary battle plan rather than our own.

In what ways has your understanding of God's kingdom changed as a result of reading Jesus' five discourses?

Which of the Beatitudes especially helps you understand how a person should live in the kingdom of God?

Which verse would you select as your "motto verse" to read several times a day and seek to put into practice during the next several weeks?

In what specific ways will you change how you live in order to carry out this part of Jesus' battle plan?

To what extent does the theme of *love God and love other people* recur in Jesus' discourses?

How might your life, and the lives of other people around you, be different if you diligently followed the commands to love that Jesus gave in his five discourses?

Which perspectives and attitudes may be hindering you from doing this?

Obviously Jesus knew that aspects of God's kingdom would thoroughly irritate some of his listeners, yet he spoke boldly and refused to compromise his message. What relevance does this have for Christians today — in our schools, neighborhoods, workplaces, and so on?

Memorize

As you go, preach this message: "The kingdom of heaven is near." Heal the sick, raise the dead, cleanse those who have leprosy, drive out demons.

Matthew 10:7–8

Day Two | Jesus Ministers to Diverse Communities

The Very Words of God

Jesus left that place and went to the vicinity of Tyre ... as soon as she heard about him, a woman whose little daughter was possessed by an evil spirit came and fell at his feet. The woman was a Greek, born in Syrian Phoenicia. She begged Jesus to drive the demon out of her daughter.... Then Jesus left the vicinity of Tyre and went through Sidon, down to the Sea of Galilee and into the region of the Decapolis.

Mark 7:24–31

Bible Discovery

Jesus Shared His Message with Everyone

Many different types of people — religious and nonreligious, Jews and Gentiles, rich and poor, farmers and merchants — populated the cities and villages around the Sea of Galilee. Although certain groups tended to live in specific areas, the Via Maris trade route brought foreign travelers into the area. In addition, people within the region traveled from one area to another in the course of their business dealings and to hear Jesus and other rabbis teach. No matter where in the region he taught, Jesus tailored his message to the beliefs and practices of his specific audience. As you study what Jesus taught in various places in Galilee, locate each area on the map found on page 121 and notice the unique message Jesus shared in that region.

The Northwestern Shore of the Sea of Galilee

Home of Orthodox Jews, this area had many synagogues. The Pharisees, who were devoted to keeping God's Torah perfectly, predominated. People there knew the Scriptures and longed for the Messiah to come and to relieve them of the burdens of taxes and their scholars' endless debates.

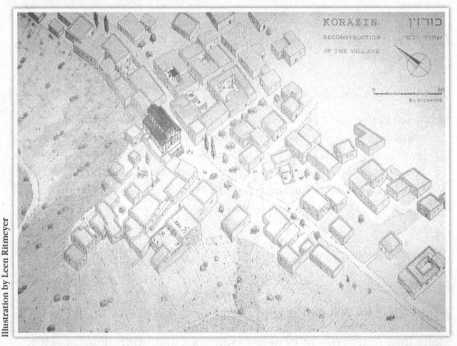

Illustration by Leen Ritmeyer

KORAZIN

1. Where was the "headquarters" of Jesus' ministry? (See Matthew 4:13 – 16.)

   Why might Jesus have picked this place to begin his teaching and choose his disciples? (See Matthew 4:17 – 22.)

   What did Jesus reveal about his kingdom that may have surprised listeners who worked very hard to obey the teachings of the Torah? (See Matthew 11:28 – 30.)

DID YOU KNOW?

A rabbi of Jesus' day would encourage his disciples to take on the "yoke of Torah," which meant to commit to obeying Torah as the rabbi interpreted and taught it. Jesus criticized some teachers of the law for making obedience to Torah excessively difficult—so burdensome that they themselves were not willing to do what they required of others (see Matthew 23:1 – 7).

Northeastern Corner of the Sea of Galilee

Gamla, which was perched on a steep mountaintop in this region, was the home of Judah of Gamla, a Pharisee who started the Zealot movement. Although the term *Zealot* technically applies to people who belonged to the movement that originated in Gamla, it is often applied to all rebels who resisted Roman authority. Zealots longed for a messiah who would raise up a great army and overthrow the Romans. Although there is no record that Jesus visited Gamla, he visited nearby towns and villages.

2. Where in the northern part of the Sea of Galilee did Jesus teach and heal, and why? (See Matthew 9:35 – 36.)

As Jesus demonstrated his miraculous power in the region, the Zealots would have seen and heard about it. What unusual request did he often make when he healed people? (See Matthew 8:1 – 4; 9:27 – 30.)

3. What did Jesus think people would do if they believed he was the messiah they envisioned? (See John 6:14 – 15.)

Which group of people would be most likely to do this?

What does this tell you about the kind of kingdom Jesus represented?

Eastern Shore of the Sea of Galilee: The Decapolis

The Decapolis was an independent region of city-states established by Alexander the Great and strengthened by the Roman conqueror Pompey. A Roman Legion was stationed in Susita of the Decapolis. For the most part, people living here were pagans who worshiped Greek and Roman gods.

4. The people of the Decapolis raised pigs, which the Jews considered to be unclean, and sacrificed pigs in their worship

SUSITA IN THE DECAPOLIS

of pagan gods, which the Jews considered to be demonic.
This is why many Jews believed that demons lived in the
Decapolis. It was not a place that religious Jews generally fre-
quented, yet Jesus went there. (See Mark 5:1 – 20.)

a. What did Jesus do when he visited the Decapolis, and
   why do you think he did this particular miracle?

b. What did Jesus tell the healed man to do, and why do
   you think his instructions differed from those he had
   given to others he had healed in the region near Gamla?

c. What impact did this miracle have on people? What impact does it have on you?

Southwestern Shore of the Sea of Galilee

Herod Antipas, who executed John the Baptist, built beautiful Tiberias, his capital city, on the southwestern shore of the Sea of Galilee. Tradition holds that religious Jews would not live here during Jesus' time because the city was built over a cemetery. The city's inhabitants were mostly secular Jews who supported Herod's dynasty, in part because of the economic and political power they enjoyed.

5. After Jesus challenged pro-Herodian religious leaders to answer whether it was lawful to heal on the Sabbath, he healed a man's shriveled hand. How did the Pharisees respond? (See Mark 3:1 – 6.)

DATA FILE
The "Way of the Sea"
During biblical times, Israel was located at the crossroads of the world. Since the Arabian desert lay between the empires of Egypt and Mesopotamia (Persia, Babylon, Assyria), the primary trade route of the civilized world passed through Israel, a narrow region of habitable land between the Mediterranean Sea and the desert to the east. This busy road, the lifeline of the trade route, was known as the Via Maris, the "Way of the Sea." God placed Israel in this land so that the world might know that he is God. (See Isaiah 43:12.)

Reflection

As he ministered throughout Galilee, Jesus demonstrated great love, compassion, and understanding of people's needs and spiritual condition. It is amazing to realize the diversity of people Jesus reached in this relatively small area that was indeed at the crossroads of the ancient world. His coming truly was the dawning of a great light, as the prophet Isaiah had said (Isaiah 9:1 – 2).

In light of the diversity of people with whom we interact in our world, why is it helpful for us to think about the different ways in which Jesus responded to the great variety of people living around the Sea of Galilee?

Which examples come to mind of people in your world who interpret Jesus through their own belief systems?

In what ways do their beliefs make it difficult for them to comprehend, or sometimes even hear, the message of the kingdom of God?

How might you present the message of Jesus in a way that might be easier for them to understand?

What can you do to keep your own biases and desires from distorting Jesus' message?

What can you learn from the account of the demoniac in Mark 5 about the importance of sharing your spiritual stories — what Jesus has done for you?

Memorize

In the future he will honor Galilee of the Gentiles, by the way of the sea, along the Jordan — The people walking in darkness have seen a great light; on those living in the land of the shadow of death a light has dawned.

Isaiah 9:1 – 2

Day Three | Jesus' Message of Repentance

The Very Words of God

After John was put in prison, Jesus went into Galilee, proclaiming the good news of God. "The time has come," he said. "The kingdom of God is near. Repent and believe the good news!"

Mark 1:14 – 15

Bible Discovery

The Burden of Those Who Refuse Jesus' Message

Many people living in Galilee and beyond witnessed Jesus' miracles, listened to his teaching, followed him, and embraced his message of the kingdom of God. Others, however, criticized his actions, rejected his teaching, and spurned his appeal to repent and experience the kingdom of God. To these, Jesus gave a strong warning.

1. For what reason did Jesus denounce Korazin, Bethsaida, and Capernaum, the cities in which he had performed most of his miracles? (See Matthew 11:20 – 24.)

   To which other cities did Jesus compare Korazin, Bethsaida, and Capernaum?

2. What would the residents of Korazin, Bethsaida, and Capernaum have known about Sodom, Tyre, and Sidon? (See Genesis 19:1 – 13; 1 Kings 11:33; 16:29 – 33; Ezekiel 16:49 – 50; 26:1 – 6; 28:1 – 7, 20 – 24; Joel 3:4 – 6; Amos 1:9 – 10.)

   What impact do you think Jesus' comparison would have made on the people of these Galilean cities who considered themselves to be obedient, God-fearing people?

3. Why was the penalty Jesus pronounced for Korazin, Bethsaida, and Capernaum more severe than that for Tyre, Sidon, and Sodom — whose inhabitants were among the most evil people of the Old Testament? (Reread Matthew 11:20 – 24.)

Reflection

It's often so much easier for us to see the need for other people to repent than it is to see our own. So while we can picture Jesus denouncing the unrepentant people of Korazin, Bethsaida, and Capernaum, it's harder to repent of our own unbelief and unfaithfulness.

> In what way(s) do Christians today, who know of the miracle of Jesus' atonement and forgiveness, commit the same sin of unrepentant unbelief that the people of Korazin, Bethsaida, and Capernaum committed?

> What would be some contemporary examples of the sin of unbelief, and what impact does it have on the message of the kingdom of God?

> How are unbelief and unfaithfulness having an impact in your life and perhaps hindering your testimony of the kingdom of God?

If you have heard about Jesus and his Word regularly at home, work, school, and/or in church, yet are not responding to him in confession and passionate obedience, how are you different from the people of Korazin, Bethsaida, and Capernaum?

If you are a Christian, what do you think your relationship should be with people who have heard all about Jesus yet refuse to repent?

What does repentance accomplish in the life of a Christian?

Do we ever outgrow our need for it?

What has happened in your life when you have tolerated sin rather than confessing it to God and turning away from it?

Memorize

I tell you that in the same way there will be more rejoicing in heaven over one sinner who repents than over ninety-nine righteous persons who do not need to repent.

Luke 15:7

Day Four | Jesus Will Return for His Beloved Bride

The Very Words of God

Therefore keep watch, because you do not know on what day your Lord will come.... The Son of Man will come at an hour when you do not expect him.

Matthew 24:42 – 44

Bible Discovery

Waiting for the Bridegroom's Return

In first-century Israel, the bride-to-be remained at her parents' home, preparing for her wedding and learning how to be a wife and mother. One day, without warning, the husband-to-be and his friends and family would arrive at her home. They would announce their arrival with singing, dancing, shouting, and maybe even by blowing a trumpet, and then take the bride to her new home. After the couple consummated their wedding, a lengthy celebration followed. It was this common marriage custom that Jesus chose to explain his relationship with his beloved bride — those who have placed their trust in him as Lord and Savior. The challenge for his followers today is to remember his future coming and to live accordingly and be ready!

1. When will Jesus come for us, and why must we always be ready for his return? (See Matthew 24:36 – 44; Mark 13:35; Luke 12:40; 1 Thessalonians 5:1 – 3; Revelation 16:15.)

2. What incentive did Jesus give for his followers always to be ready for his return in Matthew 25:1 – 13?

3. How will Jesus, our spiritual Bridegroom, announce his arrival? (See 1 Thessalonians 4:16 – 17.)

4. What can we look forward to when Jesus takes us to the new home he is preparing for us? (See Revelation 19:6 – 9; 21:2 – 5.)

Reflection

People today often minimize, or disbelieve, the fact that Jesus the Messiah will return unexpectedly to claim his beloved bride. Yet Jesus has already paid the price to make us his own. And when the Father says the time is right, Jesus will come for us. The question is, will his bride be faithful? Will she be waiting and ready for his coming?

To what extent can you comprehend Jesus' personal, deep love for you — the love a husband has for his beloved bride?

In what ways has what you have learned about first-century Jewish marriage customs helped you better understand Jesus' love and commitment to you as your "spiritual husband"?

On a scale of one (low) to ten (high), to what degree are your everyday thoughts and actions influenced by the imminent return of Jesus to take you to your new home with him?

To what extent is his promised return a source of joy for you?

How important is it that you be watchful and ready for Jesus' coming, and how prepared do you think you are?

Day Five | Be Ready When Jesus Comes Again

The Very Words of God

*Pursue righteousness, godliness, faith, love, endurance and gentleness.
Fight the good fight of the faith. Take hold of the eternal life to which you
were called when you made your good confession in the presence of many
witnesses. In the sight of God, who gives life to everything, and of Christ
Jesus, who while testifying before Pontius Pilate made the good confession,
I charge you to keep this command without spot or blame until the
appearing of our Lord Jesus Christ, which God will bring about in his own
time — God, the blessed and only Ruler, the King of kings and Lord of lords,
who alone is immortal and who lives in unapproachable light.*

1 Timothy 6:11 – 16

Bible Discovery

Prepare for His Return

Jesus is coming again, and he urges us to be ready! But what's
involved in "being ready"? Practically speaking, what are some
of the choices we must make if we truly "keep watch," if we live
expectantly as a bride-to-be preparing for her wedding? What
thoughts, attitudes, and actions should consume our every moment
if we are "engaged" to Jesus as our spiritual husband?

Carefully read each of the Bible passages on page 149 and consider what instruction the passage provides about living in
expectation of Christ's return. Then write out (1) the lifestyle
priorities addressed in the passage that we must choose in order
to prepare ourselves for Christ's return and (2) at least one practical way you can begin to live by that priority.

For example, Ephesians 5:3 indicates that certain attitudes
and behaviors are improper for God's holy people. So to be
prepared for Christ's return, we need to choose what is proper,
which means that we must turn away from every hint of impu-
rity and greed.

Scripture Text	Lifestyle Priority	Practical Step for My Life
Matt. 22:37–39		
Eph. 5:3–10		
1 Thess. 5:16–24		
1 Tim. 6:11–15		
Titus 2:11–14		
1 John 1:9		
1 John 2:3–6		
1 John 2:28		

Reflection

The Scripture passages above are just a few of many that shed light on the life God calls each of his followers to live as we wait for Jesus' return. As you think about these passages, pay special attention to ones that stood out to you. These may indicate areas where you can take steps to be better prepared for Christ's return.

Which challenges, responsibilities, and commitments are the highest priorities in your life? (Be honest!) To what extent are the biblical admonitions on page 149 included in these priorities?

In what specific way(s) are you, if you are a beloved follower of Jesus the Messiah, actively preparing for his return?

If you were to change three aspects of your life right now — actions, words, and/or thoughts — in light of the fact that Jesus may come tomorrow, what would they be?

What's keeping you from dedicating yourself to begin changing them now?

With God's help, which specific things will you start doing this week — and keep doing long term — in order to be a "bride" who is prepared, confident, and unashamed when Jesus returns?

Memorize

And now, dear children, continue in him [Jesus Christ], so that when he appears we may be confident and unashamed before him at his coming.

1 John 2:28

THE RABBI

Gamla was an isolated city situated on a steep mountain northeast of the Sea of Galilee. The mountain was so steep, even on its more gentle southern slope, that houses were built on top of one another — terraced so that the roof of one house became the "front yard" of the house above it. The northern side of the mountain was a sheer cliff.

The city was founded in about 150 BC by Jews from Babylon who returned to their homeland after the Maccabees freed the land from Seleucid Greeks. At the time of Jesus, Gamla was a city of Zealots — passionate and fiercely independent Jews who loved God and were committed to serving him and him alone. They considered violent rebellion against Rome's oppression to be their God-ordained responsibility. They eagerly awaited a messiah who would exercise political and military might.

Jesus, however, offered a different kind of freedom. But the Zealots rejected his freedom, and he wept for them as he rode into Jerusalem and saw the people waving palm branches in defiance of Rome. He knew how they would suffer because they sought the peace of an earthly kingdom rather than the peace of the heavenly kingdom.

Suffering for the Zealots came during the first Jewish revolt, which began in AD 66, years after Jesus' death and resurrection. Because Zealots from Gamla took part in the revolt, 30,000 Roman soldiers surrounded the city to put down the uprising. After the Romans breached the city wall, Gamla's inhabitants and others who had taken refuge there panicked. More than 5,000 men, women, and children perished as they jumped or pushed one another over the cliff on the mountain's north side. Then the Romans destroyed Gamla, which remains unsettled to this day. What a tragic end for people who loved God so passionately!

The remains of Gamla include a synagogue that was built as early as 100 BC, making it one of the earliest synagogues ever found. For the religious Jews of Gamla, the synagogue was a place to worship, pray, study the Torah, and understand God's will for their lives as well as a community center and school. The synagogue in Gamla is similar to other synagogues in Galilee during Jesus' time, and it gives us an opportunity to better understand how Jesus ministered as a Jewish rabbi within the Jewish community.

Surrounded by the tumultuous political backdrop of pro-Roman Herodians, religious Pharisees, pagans, and Zealots, Jesus used the teaching style of a rabbi to communicate his message. Like other rabbis, he participated in the life of the synagogue. Jesus read and interpreted the Torah and, in obedience to its commands, wore the Jewish prayer shawl with its tassels (*tsitsityot*) as a reminder of the five books of Moses (the Jews' covenant with God) and the four letters of God's sacred and holy name.

Like other rabbis, Jesus taught by example. He knew that military rebellion could never bring the Jews true freedom. So by his lifestyle he encouraged them to use a different method of influencing their culture. He healed the sick, the lame, and the blind. He blessed and forgave people whose inner hurts and brokenness led them to commit sinful acts.

Jesus' powerful message of restoration, forgiveness, and love attracted many people, but it repelled and infuriated others. It is no different today. Will we, as followers of Jesus, accept his claim to be God's Messiah and obediently pursue his way of living? Will we choose to love our enemies and care about other people more than ourselves? Will we step up to our holy calling and, by how we live and what we teach, enable other people to see the kingdom of God?

Opening Thoughts (4 minutes)

The Very Words of God

> *To the Jews who had believed him, Jesus said, "If you hold to my teaching, you are really my disciples. Then you will know the truth, and the truth will set you free."*
>
> *John 8:31–32*

Think About It

Commitment. It means different things to different people and different things in different situations. We may have commitments to tasks, relationships, causes, or goals. We often criticize other people when we feel they have taken their commitments too lightly or too seriously.

What leads us to make a commitment? What risks do we face when we are deeply committed to something? How do we know when we have "crossed the line" and become fanatical about a commitment?

DVD Teaching Notes (19 minutes)

Gamla—the home of the Zealot movement

The synagogue—center of Jewish community and religious life

Jesus the rabbi

DVD Discussion (7 minutes)

1. Look at the map below and locate Gamla. Note its proximity
    to the Sea of Galilee and the towns of Bethsaida, Capernaum,
    and Korazin, where Jesus conducted much of his ministry.

    From what you have learned during these sessions about
    Galilee, in what ways do you think Gamla was similar to
    Korazin, Capernaum, and Bethsaida?

GALILEE

In what ways do you think life in Gamla differed from life in Korazin, Capernaum, and Bethsaida?

2. Who were the Zealots, and how influential were they in Galilee? In Gamla?

What impact do you think the destruction of Gamla by the Romans had on the region?

SYNAGOGUE OF GAMLA

3. What did you learn about the importance and function of the synagogue in Jewish life at the time of Jesus?

4. In what ways was Jesus' role as a rabbi important to God's plan of redemption?

Small Group Bible Discovery and Discussion (18 minutes)

The Freedom Jesus Offered

During the course of his ministry, Jesus taught a kind of freedom that differed significantly from the freedom sought by Zealots and other people who lived in Galilee. Like other rabbis of his day, Jesus had *talmidim*, disciples who lived in a close, obedient relationship with him and who sought to live as he lived every day. Let's look at the kind of freedom he promised, the lifestyle he commanded, and what makes such a life stand out prominently in culture.

1. Who, according to Jesus, are his disciples? (See John 8:31 – 34, 36.)

    What did Jesus say his disciples would learn by following his teachings, and what would it accomplish?

What did Jesus say enslaves a person, and what makes a person truly free?

How is this freedom like or unlike the freedom that the people of Jesus' day desired, and in what way did their pre-existing ideas about freedom influence their ability to understand what he was saying?

How would you explain, in a way people in your world will understand, the freedom Jesus offers?

2. What kind of teacher of the Torah did Jesus say he would be? (See Matthew 11:28 – 30.)

What freedom would his disciples find if they took on his "yoke," meaning his teaching and example of how to obey the Torah?

How do you think Jesus' audiences — everyday people, rabbis, other religious leaders — understood and responded to this teaching?

DID YOU KNOW?
Rabbis during Jesus' time selected students, called *talmidim*, who followed their rabbi in order to learn his interpretations of the Torah and to model his obedience to God's law. A rabbi's *talmidim* were said to take on the "yoke of Torah," which meant they committed themselves to obeying Torah as the rabbi interpreted and taught it.

3. What "freedom" did Jesus demonstrate for his disciples in John 13:12 – 15, and command them to follow in John 13:34 – 35?

    Do you think Jesus' first disciples found it easy to live out the lifestyle to which he called them? Why or why not?

    How easy is it for us to live this way today?

    Why does this kind of example stand out in our culture today, just as it did during the first century?

Faith Lesson (6 minutes)

Today, Jesus invites each of us to be in relationship with him as his disciple, his *talmid*. He wants us to experience the kind of freedom that only he can provide. He challenges us to live a life of love and servanthood that will demonstrate to other people that he is the Messiah who sets his people free from the bondage of sin.

1. How is the freedom Jesus offers like or unlike the freedom you desire? Have you accepted his offer, or are you holding out for a different kind of freedom?

2. How would you describe in your own words the "yoke" that Jesus invited his disciples to take on?

3. As people look at you and your lifestyle, how obvious is it that you are (or are not) a disciple of Jesus?

    If you are a *talmid* of Jesus, what changes in thought, word, and action do you need to make so that other people will more easily recognize your relationship with him?

4. What impact does genuine love — the love of Christ that flows from his *talmidim* — have on people? Communities? Cultures? Nations?

Closing (1 minute)

Read John 13:34 - 35 together: "A new command I give you: Love one another. As I have loved you, so you must love one another. By this all men will know that you are my disciples, if you love one another." Then pray, thanking Jesus for setting you free to serve and love as he serves and loves. Invite him to teach you to obey him and to express his love to people around you. Ask him to help you be as devoted to him as his disciples were, so that people in your world will know that he is God.

Memorize

A new command I give you: Love one another. As I have loved you, so you must love one another. By this all men will know that you are my disciples, if you love one another.

John 13:34 - 35

Understanding the World in Which Jesus Lived

In-Depth Personal Study Sessions

Day One | The Lifestyle of a First-Century Rabbi

The Very Words of God

> *Now there was a man of the Pharisees named Nicodemus, a member of the Jewish ruling council. He came to Jesus at night and said, "Rabbi, we know you are a teacher who has come from God. For no one could perform the miraculous signs you are doing if God were not with him."*
>
> John 3:1 – 2

Bible Discovery

Jesus Lived and Taught as a Rabbi

Jesus' role as a first-century Jewish rabbi (teacher) provided the perfect setting in which to proclaim his message of the kingdom of God. The way Jesus lived was in many ways similar to the lifestyle and teaching practices of other rabbis who lived during that time.

1. What did many people who encountered Jesus consider him to be? (See Luke 7: 36 – 40; 12:13 – 14; 18:18; 19:39; John 3:1 – 2.)

    What do these brief examples reveal about how people viewed the rabbis? For example, to what extent were rabbis respected and by whom? How seriously did people think about a rabbi's words and heed his instruction? What did people expect of their rabbis?

THE TRUTH OF THE MATTER
To Be Called a "Rabbi"

In first-century Israel, the title *rabbi* meant "master" or "teacher." It was a term of respect or a description of activity. The position of "rabbi" didn't become an official office until after Jesus' time. Many diverse people believed Jesus to be a rabbi:

- A rich, young ruler (Matthew 19:16–22)
- Pharisees who were experts in the law (Matthew 22:34–36)
- An unnamed man in the crowd (Luke 12:13)
- Sadducees (Luke 20:27–33)
- A blind man (Mark 10:51)

2. What do the following passages of Scripture reveal about the lifestyle of rabbis who lived during the time of Jesus — what they did, how they were supported, who listened to them, how they taught, who followed them?

Scripture Text	The Rabbi's Life
Luke 8:1–3	
Matt. 26:55; Mark 6:6; Luke 4:15–22	

Matt. 13:1–3	
Matt. 11:29–30	
Matt. 10:1–14; 20:29; Luke 5:27–28; 14:25	

Reflection

At the time of Jesus, a rabbi was respected because of his knowledge and commitment to the Scriptures. A rabbi's disciples, his *talmidim*, wanted more than anything else to be like their rabbi — to know what he knew, to do what he did, to walk as he walked. Among the God-fearing Jews of Galilee, there were many rabbis and *talmidim*.

> In what way(s) was what Jesus taught similar to and different from the teachings of other rabbis? (Think particularly of the things for which Jesus was criticized.)

> Which types of people do you think were especially attracted to Jesus' teaching and why?

> How do you think other rabbis in Galilee may have felt about or responded to Jesus and his teaching?

Which characteristics and practices of first-century rabbis would easily carry over into modern culture? Which characteristics would not?

If Jesus were on earth today, *where* do you think he would teach, and *what* do you think he would teach?

How might you expect various groups of people, including religious leaders, to respond to him?

If you wanted to know what it means to be a disciple of Jesus, how would reading the Gospels (the books of Matthew, Mark, Luke, and John) help you?

Memorize

Now there was a man of the Pharisees named Nicodemus, a member of the Jewish ruling council. He came to Jesus at night and said, "Rabbi, we know you are a teacher who has come from God. For no one could perform the miraculous signs you are doing if God were not with him."

John 3:1 – 2

DATA FILE
What Is a Disciple?

The Hebrew word for *disciple* is *talmid* (plural, *talmidim*). This word stresses the relationship between rabbi (teacher or master) and disciple (student). A *talmid* of Jesus' day would give up his entire life in order to be with his teacher. The disciple didn't only seek to know what the teacher knew, as is usually the case in our educational practice today. It was not enough just to *know* what the rabbi said. Rather, the foremost goal of any *talmid* was to become *like* the rabbi and do what the rabbi did (Luke 6:40). The Pharisees, for example, knew and taught the truth (according to Matthew 23:1 – 4), but many of them were not Jesus' disciples because they did not obey God's teaching.

Jesus' disciples became like him in various ways. For example, they performed miracles, loved their enemies, and were persecuted and killed for their faith. Today, Jesus calls us to be his disciples — to know his message, to share it with others, and to model our lives after his (Matthew 28:19 – 20; John 8:31; 13:34 – 35).

Day Two | Jesus Taught in Synagogues

The Very Words of God

> *Jesus went through all the towns and villages, teaching in their synagogues, preaching the good news of the kingdom and healing every disease and sickness.*
>
> **Matthew 9:35**

Bible Discovery

Jesus Ministers to the Community of Faith

The New Testament records more than ten occasions when Jesus ministered in synagogues. Synagogue worship was an important part of the Jews' relationship to God and provided a ready platform for Jesus' teaching. Imagine Jesus standing on the *bema* (speaker's platform) reading the Torah scrolls or sitting on a stone bench or on the floor and listening to an interpretation of the text that was read. As we understand what took place in the synagogues and what role they played in Jewish life, we can better appreciate Jesus' actions and teaching there.

DATA FILE
Synagogues of Jesus' Time
Synagogues were a part of Jewish life well before Jesus' time. They began as small assemblies of people gathered for the purpose of study and prayer (perhaps as early as the time of Solomon's temple), and became particularly important during the Babylonian exile following the destruction of the first temple in Jerusalem. In Babylon, the Jews met regularly to study the Torah and reflect on their need to obey God. The synagogue developed out of these regular meetings. It provided a place for the Jewish people to assemble and

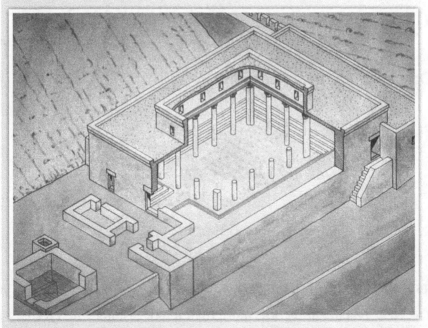

A GALILEAN SYNAGOGUE

maintain their identity in a pagan land. It became the center of Jewish social life as well as a place of study and prayer.

During the first century, the synagogue remained the focal point of Jewish community life. It served as school, meeting place, courtroom, seat of government, place of prayer, center for community celebrations, and in some cases may have provided lodging for travelers. In typical Galilean towns, the synagogue occupied a prominent place on an elevated platform in the town center or on the highest point in town, symbolizing the importance of living in God's presence.

Outside each synagogue was a *mikveh* (plural, *mikvoth*), a ritual bath where worshipers symbolically cleansed their hearts before entering the synagogue. The *mikveh* had to be hewn out of rock or placed into the ground, and the water had to be "living" — flowing freely into the *mikveh* without being drawn. This tradition was in keeping with laws of the Torah regarding contact with "unclean" things (Numbers 19), bodily fluid (Leviticus 15), or other defiling objects such as idols.

Local elders governed each synagogue, and males thirteen years old or older could belong to it. A local ruler, called the hazzan, maintained the building and organized the prayer services (Mark 5:22, 35 – 38; Luke 13:14). He often taught in the synagogue school (especially in smaller villages), announced the arrival of the Sabbath with blasts on the shofar (ram's horn) on Friday evenings, and cared for the Torah scrolls and other sacred writings.

Inside the synagogue, the leader of the service sat on a small, elevated platform on which a reading table, a menorah (a seven-branched candlestick), and a seat (sometimes referred to as Moses' seat; see Matthew 23:2) may have been placed. Members of the synagogue either sat on the floor or on stone benches or steps against the walls (the chief seats were those on the stone benches; see Matthew 23:6). Common people sat on mats on the floor, which was usually paved with flagstones (although it was sometimes dirt and in later synagogues could have been made of elaborate mosaic tiles). Torah scrolls were kept in a permanent (but portable) chest called the holy ark — after the original ark of the covenant in which Moses placed the tablets of the law.

1. In which towns and regions of Israel did Jesus teach in synagogues? (See Matthew 4:23; Mark 1:21; Luke 4:14 – 22, 44.)

   How important do you think the synagogue was to his ministry? Why?

2. What did Jesus' ministry in the synagogues involve?

Scripture Text	How Jesus Ministered
Matt. 12:9 – 13	
Luke 4:16 – 22	
Luke 4:31 – 37	
John 6:28 – 59	

3. After the Babylonians destroyed the temple in Jerusalem, the daily sacrifices ended abruptly and the Jews could no longer worship God as they had for centuries. Jewish scholars believe that Jews gathered in their homes during the exile to focus on studying God's law. What "sacrifices" other than animals are pleasing to God? (See Psalm 51:16 – 17; Isaiah 1:11 – 17.)

4. What do Galatians 6:10 and Ephesians 2:19 – 22 say about
    the community of faith, the church, that was born out of the
    synagogue?

5. What did the apostle Paul express concerning the way in
    which Christians "sacrifice" to God? (See Romans 12:1 – 2,
    9 – 21.)

HIGHLIGHTS OF SABBATH WORSHIP

- Took place on Saturday morning in the synagogue.
- Began with several blessings offered to God, followed by the *Shema*:
  "Hear, O Israel: The Lord our God, the Lord is one" (Deuteronomy 6:4).
- The person selected to read the Torah would sit on the stone "Moses'
  seat" until the *hazzan* (temple ruler) brought the Torah scrolls. Then, the
  reader would stand up to read the words of Moses (Luke 4:16 – 21).
- Different members of the synagogue community read as many as seven
  portions of the Torah.
- A selection from the Prophets was then read.
- A short sermon was offered. Interestingly, any member of the synagogue
  community could deliver the sermon. Often someone recognized for his
  wisdom and insight, or a visitor, offered the sermon. Even boys over age
  thirteen could, with permission, read or speak during the service. In this
  way, the community encouraged its youngest members to actively participate in its religious life.
- The service ended with a benediction. If a priest was present, he would
  offer the blessing of Aaron from the Torah (Numbers 6:24 – 26) at the end
  of the service. Aside from offering this blessing, priests and Levites could
  participate, but had no special role in synagogue life.

Reflection

In first-century Galilean towns, each synagogue played a key role in community life. People honored God and the Torah — his Word — and relied on it for guidance and strength in living a life of obedience to God. Through the reading of the Word of God, teaching it, and discussion on how to apply it, the synagogues influenced people's lives and shaped their future.

What level of reverence did the Galileans have for the Torah, and how does your view of the Bible compare to theirs?

Would you say that your local faith community is an essential part of your overall community's well-being? Why or why not?

How seriously do you individually and in your faith community study Scripture? Memorize it? Learn how to apply it to your daily life?

What are the consequences of your level of commitment to God's Word?

Reread Romans 12:1 - 2, 9 - 21; Psalm 51:16 - 17; and Isaiah 1:11 - 17 and review some of the ways in which you are and are not offering your body as a living sacrifice to God. Which of these descriptions stood out to you? Why? (You might use the following chart to stimulate your thinking.)

Ways to Offer Ourselves as Living Sacrifices to God	How My Thoughts and Actions Relate to These Ways
Being holy; not conforming to the world's values	
Sincerely loving and honoring other people	
Serving God	
Being joyful in hope	
Sharing with needy people	
Practicing hospitality	
Loving our persecutors	
Living in unity with others	
Being humble	
Avoiding revenge	
Living peacefully as well as we can	
Having an obedient, contrite heart	
Following God's truth	
Seeking justice	
Encouraging and defending oppressed and needy people	

DID YOU KNOW?
A Synagogue Education

According to the *Mishnah* (the written record of the oral traditions), students followed a specific educational plan. The Mishnah records what was true shortly after Jesus' time, but Jewish scholars believe it reflects what was already true in Jesus' day. Based on this, the learning of the community was passed orally, and the memorization of tradition and God's Word were essential. It appears that a typical education progressed as follows:

- At age five or six boys and girls went to school and began memorizing and studying the written Torah.
- At age twelve formal schooling ended for girls, but boys began to study the more complicated oral interpretations of the Torah.
- A boy became a religious adult at age thirteen.
- At age fifteen a gifted student might continue his studies with a local rabbi in *beth midrash* (meaning "house of study" or secondary school), where he learned to apply the Torah and oral tradition to specific situations. Other boys would begin learning their family trade.
- The most gifted students would travel with famous itinerant rabbis, learning to understand and apply Torah and oral tradition in daily situations and seeking to "become like their rabbis."
- A student demonstrated his full ability as a rabbi at age thirty.

By the time a student reached adulthood, he knew most Scriptures by heart and could tell whether someone quoted them correctly. Thus Jesus, in keeping with his culture, could say, "It is written . . . ," and know that his audience would recognize an accurate quotation.

Day Three | The Message of Jesus, the Rabbi

The Very Words of God

I have not come to call the righteous, but sinners to repentance.

Luke 5:32

Bible Discovery

Jesus Addressed the Important Questions of His World

Jesus lived and taught in towns and villages near the most heavily traveled road of the ancient world, the Via Maris (also called the "Way of the Sea"). In fulfillment of the ancient prophecies, he chose Capernaum, a stop on Via Maris, to be his "hometown" during his ministry (Matthew 4:12 - 16). Wherever he went, he spoke to a wide variety of people about such things as what the kingdom of heaven was like, who he was, the importance of repentance, what it meant to truly obey God, and how to live in such a way that the world would know that God was God.

1. What was the basic theme of Jesus' message? How much interest did it generate in his world, and why? (See Matthew 4:17; Mark 1:15; Luke 13:1 - 5.)

2. For what did Jesus strongly condemn teachers of the law and some Pharisees? (See Matthew 15:1 - 20; 23:1 - 7, 13 - 28.)

    Why do you think Jesus was so offended by their behavior and by the message they were sending to the people?

    What alternative message did Jesus offer? (See Matthew 11:28 - 30.)

3. Describe the astounding event that occurred one Sabbath in Nazareth when it was time for Jesus to read his assigned portion from the Prophets. (See Luke 4:14 – 21.)

   Why was this important news for the people of Jesus' day?

4. What did Jesus teach about issues of what we would call "social justice"? (See Matthew 6:3; 25:31 – 40; Luke 14:13 – 14; 18:20 – 25.)

   How important do you think social justice was to the people of Jesus' world, and why?

   Why was the way in which Jesus presented this message important for his audience?

5. What did Jesus say was required of those who would follow him? (See Matthew 16:24 – 28.)

   How would this message have touched the concerns of various people in his audience such as the Zealots, Sadducees, Pharisees, and everyday God-fearing people of Galilee?

DID YOU KNOW?
Understanding a Great Miracle

During Jesus' time, Jewish men wore two garments: a light tunic and a heavy mantle worn over the tunic (*tallit* in Hebrew). Attached to the corners of the *tallit* were the tassels (*tsitsityot*) that God had commanded the Israelites to wear (Numbers 15:37–41; Deuteronomy 22:12). The tassels reminded people of their obligations to God to keep all of his commandments, were intended to direct other people to God when the Messiah came, and reminded people that God was with his people. (The hem also communicated the wearer's status or rank.) One of the threads on each tassel had to be blue, a reminder that the Israelites were royalty because they were a "kingdom of priests."

According to Jewish tradition, the Messiah would have "healing" in his "wings" as represented by the tassels (Malachi 4:2). This tradition helps us understand the story of the diseased woman who reached out to grasp the hem—the tassel—of Jesus' mantle (Matthew 9:20–22; Luke 8:40–48). Her action demonstrated genuine faith (Mark 5:34). By grasping the tassel of Jesus' garment, she was affirming the prophet Zechariah's message that God was with him (Zechariah 8:23) and that he was truly the Messiah.

In this case, as in others recorded in Scripture, faith was essential to God's willingness to work his power (Matthew 9:29–30; Mark 10:52; Matthew 13:58). By grasping Jesus' hem, the ailing, "unclean" (Numbers 5:1–2), and nameless woman demonstrated faith in who Jesus was and what he could do for her. God in turn released his healing power and performed a miracle.

6. Much of what Jesus did was like other rabbis of his day, including his wearing of tassels as instructed in Numbers 15:37–41. According to Jewish tradition, however, what would be unique about the tassels of the Messiah? (See Zechariah 8:23; Malachi 4:2.)

What message did Jesus clearly convey to the ailing woman who touched his clothing and was healed? (See Mark 5:24 – 34.)

Reflection

When Jesus taught, whether by word or example, he did not intend for his listeners to simply store away intellectual truth. Rather, he challenged people to become like him, to actively apply the truths he taught in life-changing, culture-impacting ways.

What have you learned from the teachings of Jesus that makes a difference in your life?

About repentance and God's forgiveness of your sin?

About your most important priority in life?

About how you relate to other people, what you expect of them, and how deeply you love and care for their well-being?

About Jesus' power to make a difference in the lives of individual people and the world in which they live?

What are you still learning and seeking to understand about what it means to follow Jesus and live as he lived?

Memorize

With many similar parables Jesus spoke the word to them, as much as they could understand. He did not say anything to them without using a parable. But when he was alone with his own disciples, he explained everything.

Mark 4:33 – 34

Day Four | Jesus' Teachings vs. Zealot Teachings

The Very Words of God

Phinehas son of Eleazar, the son of Aaron, the priest, has turned my anger away from the Israelites; for he was as zealous as I am for my honor among them, so that in my zeal I did not put an end to them. Therefore tell him I am making my covenant of peace with him. He and his descendants will have a covenant of a lasting priesthood, because he was zealous for the honor of his God and made atonement for the Israelites.

Numbers 25:11 – 13

Bible Discovery

Obey No One But God!

Jesus conducted his ministry near the city of Gamla, home of the Zealots. Like them, Jesus was totally and passionately committed to serving God. He addressed issues in which they were passionately interested. Yet his message about God's kingdom stood in stark contrast to their message, which advocated a violent overthrow of Roman oppression.

1. What did the devil tempt Jesus to do regarding God's kingdom? (See Matthew 4:8 - 10.)

   What was Jesus' commitment, and how was it like or unlike the commitment of the Zealots?

   What does Jesus' response to the devil reveal about his desire to establish an earthly kingdom, and how was that desire like or unlike the desire of the Zealots?

2. As you read each of the following teachings of Jesus, consider how a Zealot might have received it. What do you think would have offended them? With which teachings would they have eagerly agreed? What might they have found confusing?

Scripture Text	How the Zealots Are Likely to Have Received Jesus' Teaching
Matt. 5:3 – 12	
Matt. 5:38 – 42	
Matt. 5:43 – 44	

DATA FILE
Who Were the Zealots?

About 45 BC, a Jewish patriot named Hezekiah led a band of freedom fighters against the Romans and their supporters. Herod the Great captured Hezekiah and executed him, as he did to thousands of like-minded Jews during his reign. Although devout Jews continued to bitterly oppose Roman rule and taxation, there was no widespread resistance movement until Judea was officially incorporated into the Roman Empire in AD 6. At that time, Judah of Gamla, the son of Hezekiah, urged violent resistance. Supported by a popular Pharisee named Zadok, also from Galilee, Judah led a revolt. Judah was killed, his followers were scattered, and the Zealot movement began.

The term *Zealot* technically applies to a person who belonged to the party or "philosophy" that began in Gamla, but it often is applied to all Jewish rebels who resisted Roman authority. For generations, the Zealots violently resisted the emperor's authority. They longed for a messiah who would raise up a great army, destroy their Roman overlords, and reestablish Jewish rule in Israel.

The Zealots based their zeal for God on the action of Phinehas, Aaron's grandson, who used a spear to defend God's name (Numbers 25:7 – 13). The Zealots interpreted this action to be a divine command to use violent action to defend God's name. This belief led to a long history of violent acts against Rome and brutal conflict between the Zealots and the Jews whom they believed cooperated with the pagan empire.

The Zealots' creed can be summarized as follows:

- There is only one God—The Zealots interpreted Exodus 20:3, "You shall have no other gods," to mean that no one other than God could be acknowledged as king.
- Israel is to serve God alone.
- The Torah and other writings of the Hebrew Bible are the only guide to righteous living—The Zealots lived in strict conformity to the Torah.
- Neither Rome nor Herod is a legitimate authority—People are to use every means possible, including violence, to resist earthly authority.

continued on next page . . .

- Serving the Roman emperor in any way—whether in worship, slavery, or by paying taxes—is apostasy against God.
- Serving Rome, whether by choice or as a slave, violates God's supreme authority.
- God is on our side, so we will triumph in the end—This belief led to the Zealots' reputation for incredible bravery and tolerance for suffering.
- The Scriptures promise that the coming Anointed One will be a great military leader and king, like King David was.

3. Why was paying taxes to Caesar an issue for both the pro-Roman Herodians and the Jewish Zealots? How did Jesus answer the loaded question he was asked about paying taxes, and how did his answer satisfy, or not satisfy, both groups? (See Matthew 22:15 – 22; Mark 12:13 – 17.)

4. The word used to describe Barabbas in Luke 23:13 – 25 is the same word used to mean *Zealot*. What was the irony in the demands of the Jewish rulers and in Pilate's decision regarding Jesus?

DID YOU KNOW?

One of the men Jesus chose to be a disciple was Simon the Zealot (Mark 3:13 – 19). We do not know whether Simon gave up his support for Zealot tactics after joining Jesus, but the disciples' tendency to see the kingdom of God as a political entity may indicate Zealot influence. Some scholars believe that the reference to Simon as a "Zealot" meant simply that he was zealous. That perspective, although possible, is unlikely.

5. Note Jesus' actions recorded in Mark 11:15 – 18 (see also Matthew 21:12 – 17; Luke 19:45 – 47).

What do you think the Zealots thought about what Jesus did?

When, in our lives, do you think such actions might be justified?

Reflection

Although some people are critical of the Zealots for choosing a militaristic stand against Rome, we can also learn from their vibrant passion for Scripture and unyielding obedience to God.

What do you think *total commitment to serving God* looks like in your world?

Where does true passion for God come from?

What do you do to feed your zeal for God and your total commitment to follow Jesus?

THE ZEALOT MOVEMENT

HASIDIM

Called the "Pious Ones," they resisted Hellenism by being totally devoted to Torah. They fought with Judah and the Maccabees against the Syrian Greeks (Seleucids) in 167 BC.

The Hasmonaeans, the Maccabees' descendants, became as Hellenistic as the Seleucid Greeks.

Hasidim becomes two movements.

PHARISEES

- Resist Hellenism and the pagan worldview
- Totally devoted to Torah

ZEALOTS

- Resist Hellenism and the pagan worldview
- Totally devoted to Torah
- Were terrorists

ZEALOTS

Hezekiah
- Resisted Rome and Herod (47 BC)
- Was executed by Herod

Judah of Gamla
- Attacked Sepphoris in 4 BC to gain control of its arsenal
- Founded Zealot party with Zadok the Pharisee in AD 6, at the time of the census
- Was probably killed by Herod Antipas (see Acts 5:37)
- Beliefs:
    1. God alone may rule Israel
    2. Pay taxes to no one but God
    3. Slavery is worse than death

Sons of Judah

Jacob
- Crucified for terrorism in AD 48

Simeon
- Crucified for terrorism in AD 48

Yair

Grandsons of Judah

Eleazar Ben Yair
- Son of Yair
- Commander of Masada
- Commited suicide in AD 73

Menahem
- Leader of a revolt in Jerusalem
- Killed by opponents in AD 66

Which aspects of the Zealots' belief system might you admire and perhaps apply to your life?

In which area(s) of life are you zealous for God, and in which area(s) are you less than committed to him?

How do you decide which are the right things to be zealous for and which are not?

DATA FILE
The End of the Zealots

The Zealot minority, although certainly influential, did not have the means to defeat the Roman Empire. Having rejected the kingdom and peace that Jesus offered, they came to a tragic end:

- Judah of Gamla, the movement's founder, was executed. His sons, Jacob and Simeon, were crucified in approximately AD 48.
- Menahem, a grandson of Judah whom some believed to be the Messiah, seized Masada in AD 66 during the first true military action of the Jewish revolt. (The Roman weapons in Masada equipped the Zealots.) Another Zealot later murdered Menahem.
- John of Gischala, a Zealot, defended Jerusalem and the Temple Mount until the Romans conquered the city.
- In AD 73, the Romans laid siege to Masada. Eleazar Ben Yair, another grandson of Judah of Gamla, held out until there was no more hope. Then the last remaining Zealots committed mass suicide.

How can you give total allegiance to Jesus and still serve human rulers?

Would you be willing to give your life for your spiritual beliefs as the Zealots did?

What can you learn from Jesus' teaching and example about relating to people around you who are highly motivated but have misguided ideologies?

Memorize

It is fine to be zealous, provided the purpose is good, and to be so always and not just when I am with you.

Galatians 4:18

Day Five | Misunderstandings About Jesus and His Kingdom

The Very Words of God

When Jesus came to the region of Caesarea Philippi, he asked his disciples, "Who do people say the Son of Man is?" They replied, "Some say John the Baptist; others say Elijah; and still others, Jeremiah or one of the prophets." "But what about you?" he asked. "Who do you say I am?" Simon Peter answered, "You are the Christ, the Son of the living God."

Matthew 16:13–16

Bible Discovery

People Heard, But They Did Not Understand

No matter how much he taught or how carefully he explained himself, people still misunderstood who Jesus was and what he was saying about his kingdom. Sometimes they genuinely wanted to understand, but couldn't see beyond their own expectations. Sometimes what Jesus taught was confusing in light of what they understood of Scripture. Sometimes they simply rejected his testimony. Sometimes they lacked the faith to believe the truth.

1. Note what the following Scripture passages reveal about how people misunderstood Jesus and his kingdom.

   The disciples (see Matthew 26:47 – 51; Mark 10:35 – 45)

   The Romans (see John 18:33 – 37)

   The crowd in the garden of Gethsemane (see Matthew 26:55 – 56)

2. The Romans apparently feared that Jesus was a Zealot. Look up the passages below and on page 186 to find evidence that could have raised their suspicions.

Scripture Text	Was He a Zealot?
Matt. 2:1 – 9	
Mark 3:13 – 18	

Mark 11:15–18	
John 12:12–15	

3. To clarify what his kingdom was about, what did Jesus say to Pilate, who no doubt wondered if Jesus was the political-military king whom the Zealots awaited? (See John 18:36.)

4. When Jesus appeared to his disciples after his resurrection, what did they ask him that reflected the ideology of the Zealots? (See Acts 1:6.)

Reflection

When people misunderstand us, we often react. We may become irritated, angry, or defensive. We may "write off" those who disagree with us or ignore them. Or we may challenge them in an effort to prove that what they say and think about us is not true. Jesus, however, responded differently.

When Jesus thought about what would happen to his people because they refused to recognize that he was the Messiah, he wept and said, "If you, even you, had only known on this day what would bring you peace — but now it is hidden from your eyes. The days will come upon you when your enemies will build an embankment against you and encircle you and hem you in on every side. They will dash you to the ground, you and the children within your walls. They will not leave one stone on another, because you did not recognize the time of God's coming to you" (Luke 19:42 – 44).

Why do you think Jesus felt such compassion for people who rejected him and his kingdom?

> How deeply do you feel compassion for people who refuse to recognize the truth of Jesus?

> If Jesus were to come into your world today, instead of 2,000 years ago, for whom would he weep and why?

In what way(s) might your response to Jesus and his kingdom be similar to the responses of the first-century Jews?

> For example, how might your expectations of the Messiah and his kingdom influence your ability to recognize who Jesus really is and the true nature of God's kingdom?

> How might your preconceived ideas be affecting your interpretations of Jesus' teachings and causing you to miss his message?

How patient are you when God's plans seem to unfold in a different manner from what you desire?

Memorize

In them is fulfilled the prophecy of Isaiah: "You will be ever hearing but never understanding; you will be ever seeing but never perceiving. For this people's heart has become calloused; they hardly hear with their ears, and they have closed their eyes. Otherwise they might see with their eyes, hear with their ears, understand with their hearts and turn, and I would heal them."

Matthew 13:14 – 15

LANGUAGE OF CULTURE

Jesus grew up in Nazareth, a village of a few hundred inhabitants in lower Galilee. Although we may picture Nazareth as a rural, out-of-the-way retreat from the world, it was not. A main branch of the Via Maris, the world's international trade route that linked Egypt with Rome and the empires to the east, passed nearby. A mere three miles north of Nazareth, Herod Antipas, a son of Herod the Great, built Sepphoris to be the administrative capital of his kingdom.

Sepphoris was a booming metropolis built on a hilltop. It could be seen for miles and, according to tradition, looked like a bird perched on the hill. Sepphoris, in fact, is the Greek translation of the Hebrew word *zippori*, which means "bird." This sprawling city covered as many as 500 acres and housed as many as 25,000 to 30,000 people. It had all the trappings of a modern, wealthy city of the Roman Empire. It boasted an elaborate water system with a cistern a thousand feet long. Rich villas with mosaic floors lined its modern streets. Herod's palace was magnificent. A colonnaded street led to the forum. Its cultural amenities included a gymnasium and a theater that could seat more than 4,000 people.

On another hill stood the village of Nazareth, where Jesus participated in a very different lifestyle. After receiving his basic education and traveling to Jerusalem for his first Passover, Jesus began to learn a trade from his father, who was a *tekton* (Matthew 13:55). The Greek word *tekton*, which is usually translated as "carpenter," actually means "a craftsman who builds." Although we typically picture Jesus as a carpenter who worked with wood, the building materials of Israel were primarily rocks and cut stones. So Jesus probably worked more as a stonemason than he did with wood. In fact, Jesus may have helped construct buildings in Sepphoris, most of which were made of local limestone and imported marble.

As he traveled and taught throughout Galilee, Jesus ministered to the needs of everyday fishermen, farmers, and tradesmen, but he also interacted with and ministered to wealthy and influential people. For example, he shared meals and had discussions with religious leaders. Joanna, the wife of Cuza (the minister of finance for Herod Antipas), used her own funds to support the ministry of Jesus and his disciples. And people accused Jesus of befriending tax collectors, who were administrative officials in the upper echelon of first-century society in Israel. Although he spoke out against the oppressive use of wealth, Jesus appreciated wealthy people who used their wealth as a tool to advance the kingdom of God.

Jesus understood the culture of his day. He knew the day-to-day experiences, concerns, and joys of farmers, influential leaders, lepers, devout Jews, blind men, and many others, which enabled him to minister effectively to them. Instead of isolating himself from people, he interacted with them. Consequently, he knew the images, tools, and concepts he could use to effectively communicate God's truth to his diverse audiences.

Many of the word pictures Jesus used came from the agricultural world of his time, particularly Galilee. When he taught, he used images from farming, fishing, and shepherding. He used images from the world of religion — both Jewish and pagan. He also used word pictures drawn from aristocratic society — the world of culture, wealth, tax collectors, politics, royalty, and the theater. He was familiar enough with the sophisticated, Hellenistic culture to use slices from it as illustrations. Thus, he could communicate clearly to those in his audience who knew that world. Because Jesus could speak the language of his culture, he taught clearly and powerfully to a wide variety of people. By communicating through the images of the culture, he made his message known.

Opening Thoughts (4 minutes)

The Very Words of God

> *Though I am free and belong to no man, I make myself a slave to everyone, to win as many as possible. To the Jews I became like a Jew, to win the Jews. To those under the law I became like one under the law (though I myself am not under the law), so as to win those under the law. To those not having the law I became like one not having the law (though I am not free from God's law but am under Christ's law), so as to win those not having the law. To the weak I became weak, to win the weak. I have become all things to all men so that by all possible means I might save some.*

> *1 Corinthians 9:19–22*

Think About It

Identify some groups of people within your culture who have diverse life experiences or differing beliefs and, therefore, don't "speak the same language" or might have difficulty understanding one another.

What is it like trying to communicate with someone who has such vastly different experiences and perceptions about life that you keep "missing" each other and can't seem to understand each other's perspective? What can be done to try to make a "connection" in a situation like this?

DVD Teaching Notes (21 minutes)

Sepphoris, a city of the Herod Dynasty

Jesus:

A *tekton* of Nazareth

Understanding his culture

Impacting his world

DVD Discussion (7 minutes)

1. Look at the maps titled "Kingdom of the Herods" and "Gali-lee" on page 193. Note the specific territories for which each of Herod's immediate successors was responsible and the locations of Nazareth and Sepphoris. In what ways do you think growing up so close to Sepphoris may have benefited Jesus and his ministry?

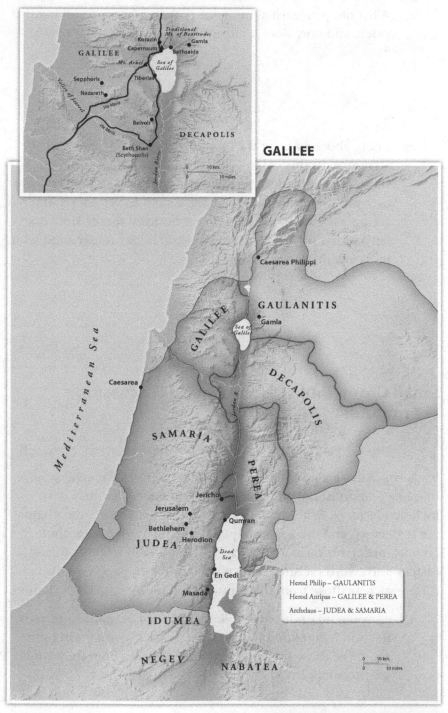

GALILEE

KINGDOM OF THE HERODS

Herod Philip – GAULANITIS

Herod Antipas – GALILEE & PEREA

Archelaus – JUDEA & SAMARIA

2. What did you learn about Jesus' vocation from watching this video, and how does it change your image of what he was like?

3. Think about some of the quotes from Jesus' teaching that were read in this video — parables about kings and their subjects, comments about actors and tax collectors. Did you ever picture Jesus being in a place such as Sepphoris, interacting with the kinds of people who lived there? How does having that picture in mind help you better understand who Jesus is and what he taught?

Small Group Bible Discovery and Discussion (17 minutes)

Jesus Taught through the "Language" of His Culture

Jesus was a master teacher. He was able to adjust his teaching so that he communicated effectively with audiences that may have included farmers, fishermen, laborers, educated people, merchants, tax collectors, and the ruling upper class. And he did so without compromising his message! Often he illustrated his points by using images and "word pictures" that were familiar to people in his culture — such as those from the theater, agriculture, and construction.

1. As you read each of the following passages, notice the activities and images that Jesus used. Pay special attention to the source of these images and the people to whom they would best communicate.

Jesus' Teachings	The Activities and Images Jesus Used	The People Who Would Understand These Images
Matt. 6:1–2, 5, 16–18		
Matt. 12:33–35		
Matt. 13:47–50		
Luke 11:11–13		
Luke 15:4–7		

2. As you read the passages above, what stood out to you about the way Jesus understood and related to his world — even aspects of it in which he would not have been directly involved?

How important is it to understand our culture well in order to minister to people and reach them with the message of Christ?

3. How might you use what is happening in various segments of your culture to better communicate God's message to people in your everyday world?

How, for example, might you use such diverse images as the paparazzi, national elections, illegal immigrants, text messaging, daycare centers, or environmental activism to teach people in your world about the kingdom of God?

DID YOU KNOW?

Jesus used the people, events, places, and activities of his time as object lessons, parables, and metaphors in his teaching. That was the traditional Jewish way. The people of the ancient Near East generally expressed their ideas in concrete language, using "word pictures" and stories to convey their views. In contrast, the Greeks thought and taught abstractly. Theory, definition, and logical systems were important to them.

Faith Lesson (5 minutes)

Clearly Jesus understood the culture, language, and people of his day, and he used that knowledge with power. Without modifying or changing God's message, Jesus found ways to communicate in a "language" of words and ideas that people of his culture spoke and understood. He used the gifts and abilities he had in order to effectively communicate his message of repentance and salvation to everyone he met. In so doing, he made a lasting impact for God.

1. In what ways have you spoken a "language" that is foreign to the secular culture around you when you have tried to communicate the gospel message to other people, and what has been the result?

2. In what ways are you effectively using your knowledge and understanding of secular culture to communicate God's truths to people?

What more do you need to learn about your culture in order to better communicate with people? Do you need, for example, to learn more about the activities of teenagers in your neighborhood? The environmental concerns of people in your region? The celebrations of particular ethnic groups in your city?

3. As you think of ways to communicate the gospel message to your culture, which messages will most effectively address the issues that concern them, the trends that influence them, the passions that drive them, and the fears that haunt them?

4. Jesus adjusted his teaching to the worldview of his audience without compromising his message. Can you think of a way in which you could tailor how you share God's truths to people at work? In your neighborhood? In your family? To children? To someone of a different race or ethnic group?

DATA FILE
Sepphoris: A Window into Jesus' World
Sepphoris, like many cities of its day, had a tumultuous history:

- When Rome first invaded Israel, the Roman commander Pompey designated Sepphoris to be the district capital of Galilee.
- Dating from at least the Hasmonaean period, the city was perched on top of a high hill surrounded by fertile, farm-dotted valleys.
- The inhabitants of the city resisted Herod the Great, however, so he slaughtered them in 37 BC and destroyed their city.
- People rebuilt Sepphoris and, led by the Zealots, its inhabitants revolted against Rome following Herod the Great's death in 4 BC.
- Roman troops conquered and destroyed the city again.
- When Herod Antipas became king of Galilee, he began rebuilding Sepphoris as his capital.

Crowned by Herod's elaborate palace, Sepphoris was home to one of the largest theaters of the first century. The city was laid out in the latest Roman pattern with a colonnaded street leading to the forum. It also featured a gymnasium, an elaborate water system, and probably a bathing complex. Just three miles away, in the humble village of Nazareth, lived a Jewish boy — a builder by trade — who became known as Jesus of Nazareth. Beautiful and

SEPPHORIS: BIRD ON A HILL

exciting Sepphoris, with its Hellenistic ideas, wealth, and power certainly impacted Nazareth and exposed Jesus to secular culture at a relatively young age.

Closing (1 minute)

Read 2 Corinthians 4:2 together: "We do not use deception, nor do we distort the word of God. On the contrary, by setting forth the truth plainly we commend ourselves to every man's conscience in the sight of God." Then pray, asking God to give you a heart that longs to share his message of salvation with others. Ask him to help you learn to communicate his message in a way that people in your culture, people who may not be like you at all, will understand.

Memorize

> *We do not use deception, nor do we distort the word of God. On the contrary, by setting forth the truth plainly we commend ourselves to every man's conscience in the sight of God.*
>
> **2 Corinthians 4:2**

Understanding the World in Which Jesus Lived

In-Depth Personal Study Sessions

Day One | Jesus and the Herods

The Very Words of God

> At that time some Pharisees came to Jesus and said to him, "Leave this place and go somewhere else. Herod wants to kill you." He replied, "Go tell that fox, 'I will drive out demons and heal people today and tomorrow, and on the third day I will reach my goal.' In any case, I must keep going today and tomorrow and the next day — for surely no prophet can die outside Jerusalem!"
>
> *Luke 13:31–33*

Bible Discovery

Jesus Interacts with the Rulers of His World

From his birth until his death, Jesus' life on earth was intertwined with that of the Herod dynasty — Herod the Great, Herod Archelaus, Herod Antipas. Although Jesus only met one of the Herods — Herod Antipas — face-to-face, he certainly knew enough about them to make subtle references to them in his teaching.

1. How did Herod the Great respond to the birth of Jesus, the "king of the Jews"? (See Matthew 2:1–8, 12–18.)

THE HEROD FAMILY TREE

Antipater (Idumaean)

HEROD THE GREAT

- Effective administrator, cruel, supported by Rome
- Visited by wise men, killed Bethlehem babies
- Greatest builder the ancient Near East ever knew
- Died in 4 BC
- Had 10 wives, three of whom were:

Cleopatra	Miriam	Malthace
PHILIP	**ANTIPAS**	**ARCHELAUS**

PHILIP	ANTIPAS	ARCHELAUS
• Effective, popular king • Ruled north and east of Galilee • Built Caesarea Philippi *(Luke 3:1)*	• Effective king • Ruled Galilee and Perea • Killed John the Baptist • Built Tiberias and Sepphoris • Tried Jesus before crucifixion *(Matthew 14:1–12; Luke 3:19; 9:7–9; 13:32; 23:7–12)*	• Poor ruler, deposed by Romans • Ruled Judea • Mary and Joseph settle in Nazareth to avoid him *(Matthew 2:22)*

HEROD AGRIPPA I

(Grandson of Herod the Great)

- King of Judea
- Killed James, put Peter in prison
- Struck down by an angel

(Acts 12:1–24)

AGRIPPA II	DRUSILLA	BERNICE
	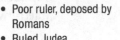 *(Sisters of Agrippa II)*	
• King of Judea • Paul defends his faith before him *(Acts 25:13–26:32)*	• Married Felix, the Roman governor *(Acts 24:24)*	• With her brother at Paul's defense *(Acts 25:13)*

2. When Joseph moved his family back to Israel, what caused him to bypass Bethlehem and settle in Nazareth, and why was this a significant move? (See Matthew 2:19 – 23.)

3. The lives of Herod Antipas (builder of Sepphoris) and Jesus intertwined. They even met face-to-face. Take a closer look at the ways in which their paths crossed.

   a. After Herod Antipas had John the Baptist killed, what impact did Jesus' ministry have on him and why? (See Matthew 14:1 – 5; Mark 6:14 – 20; Luke 9:7 – 9.)

   b. What did Herod Antipas want to do about Jesus? (See Luke 13:31.)

   c. What great irony concerning the connections between Herod Antipas and Jesus is revealed in Luke 8:1 – 3?

   d. When Pilate sent Jesus to Herod Antipas, how did they respond to each other? (See Luke 23:8 – 11.)

DID YOU KNOW?

In Jewish culture, the fox was sometimes compared to a lion. The fox was small and weak, although he might act like a powerful lion. Whereas great people are like lions in that they make good on their talk because they are truly strong, petty nobodies who put on airs and pretend to be greater than they are resemble foxes. A "fox" is someone who acts big and talks big but is really a "nobody."* Jesus may also have been referring to the fact that Herod was only a tetrarch, not a king.

*From an article entitled: "That Small Fry Herod Antipas, or When a Fox Is Not a Fox" by Randall Buth.

4. When Pharisees warned Jesus that Herod wanted to kill him, what did Jesus say about Herod and about being in control of doing what God had called him to do? (See Luke 13:31 – 33.)

5. How did the Herodians, the aristocratic Jews who supported Herod, and some of the Pharisees respond to Jesus? Why? (See Matthew 22:15 – 22; Mark 3:1 – 6; John 11:45 – 53.)

PROFILE OF A DYNASTY
The Legacy of Herod the Great

Few families in history have come as close to Jesus' message, yet remained so distant from it, as the Herods. Many members of this ruling family knew of Jesus and his followers, yet persecuted them to the point of death. Did the Herod family, descended from Esau and Edom, simply fulfill the ancient prophecies (Genesis 25:23; Numbers 24:15–19; Obadiah 1–21)?

Ruler	Notable Deeds	Last Days
Antipas: ruled Galilee and Perea 40+ years	Brought peace and prosperity; sensitive to Jewish religion yet married brother Philip's wife; built Sepphoris and Tiberias; had John the Baptist beheaded; met Jesus and plotted his death; Jesus openly criticized him	Herod Agrippa accused him of a plot; Caligula (new emperor) exiled him and claimed his property; disappeared from history
Archelaus: ruled Judea, Samaria, Idumaea 10 years	Killed families of Jewish delegations who had gone to Rome to oppose him; known for his bloodthirstiness and evil qualities, leading Joseph to settle in Nazareth rather than Bethlehem	Exiled to Gaul, then disappeared from history
Philip: ruled area north and east of the Sea of Galilee 37 years	A just ruler who governed mostly Gentiles; peace-loving; established his capital at Caesarea Philippi; married Salome, daughter of Herodias, whose dance led to John the Baptist's execution	Died of natural causes at end of his reign
Agrippa I: ruled area north and east of Sea of Galilee, Judea 8 years	Grandson of Herod the Great; ruled a large area; sought to stop Jesus' followers; killed James and imprisoned Peter and other disciples	An angel of God struck him down; he was eaten up by worms and died
Agrippa II: ruled small portion of his father's region; had limited rule in Jerusalem	Advanced Hellenistic culture; heard Paul's stirring presentation of the gospel in Caesarea, but was not persuaded	Was wounded fighting for Rome against the Zealots at Gamla, but specifics of his death are not known

Reflection

The dynasty of Herod was a threat to Jesus' life and ministry from his birth until long after his death. Although the Herods appeared to be far more powerful than Jesus, he never surrendered to them his passion to accomplish his Father's will. Even when he was brought as a prisoner before Herod, Jesus remained unmoved by what was being done to him (Luke 23:1 – 12).

> When you face pressure from other people to change your values, abandon your beliefs, or take a different course of action, how does it help you to realize that despite appearances, Jesus was far more powerful than the Herods?

> After John's death, Herod Antipas became confused about Jesus' identity and actually feared him.

> Why do you think some people are confused by who Jesus is? What keeps them from recognizing his true identity?

> For which reasons do you think Herod was afraid of Jesus, and how was his fear like or unlike what causes people today to fear Jesus?

> As much as he feared Jesus, Herod Antipas was also fascinated by him.

> Why do you think Herod asked Jesus so many questions?

What do you think he hoped to gain by seeing Jesus perform a miracle?

Today, as was true in Jesus' day, people may know about Jesus and may even see his transforming power at work, yet do not believe in him.

What is it about Jesus that fascinates people today?

When a person's interest in Jesus does not lead to faith, what is keeping that person from believing in Jesus?

Why is it important to respond positively to Jesus when you have the opportunity?

Memorize

See to it, brothers, that none of you has a sinful, unbelieving heart that turns away from the living God.... As has just been said, "Today, if you hear his voice, do not harden your hearts as you did in the rebellion."

Hebrews 3:12, 15

Day Two | Cultural Images in Jesus' Teaching

The Very Words of God

> *As John's disciples were leaving, Jesus began to speak to the crowd about John: "What did you go out into the desert to see? A reed swayed by the wind? If not, what did you go out to see? A man dressed in fine clothes? No, those who wear fine clothes are in kings' palaces. Then what did you go out to see? A prophet? Yes, I tell you, and more than a prophet."*

> *Matthew 11:7 – 9*

Bible Discovery

Jesus Puts His Cultural Awareness to Use

Jesus was not wealthy, nor did he wield political power, but he was familiar with what was happening in his world. He knew enough about historical events, including those of the Herod family, to use such knowledge effectively in his teaching. As you consider the following questions, think of how the audience may have responded when Jesus patterned his teaching after real life. How did the fact that Jesus used vivid word pictures and spoke in parables that were so similar to real life help his audience to understand his teaching?

1. Read Luke 19:11 – 27 and note the parallels between Jesus' parable about the man of noble birth and the widely known facts concerning Herod Archelaus.

The Facts in Jesus' Parable	The True Life of Herod Archelaus
Luke 19:12	Archelaus, a son of Herod the Great, went to Rome to request more land to govern than his father had bequeathed in his will.
Luke 19:14	Jews from Judea and Jerusalem sent a delegation to Rome to request that someone other than Archelaus govern them.
Luke 19:27	When Archelaus returned from Rome, he executed the Jews who had gone to Rome, killed their families, and confiscated their property.

How attentive do you think Jesus' audience was as they listened to this parable?

2. Compare Jesus' teaching in Luke 14:31 – 33 with a widely known fact concerning Herod Antipas. How well do you think Jesus made his point to his audience?

The Observation in Jesus' Teaching	The True Life of Herod Antipas
Luke 14:31 – 33	After divorcing his wife, daughter of King Aretas of Nabatea, Herod had to defend himself against the army of Aretas and lost.

3. When Jesus was teaching his disciples about how he wanted them to serve others, what did he say about the politicians of his day to make his point? (See Matthew 20:25 – 28.)

4. In Matthew 23:23 – 28, which image of the theater does Jesus use to strongly condemn the insincerity of certain Pharisees and teachers of the law?

Notice the other visual images Jesus uses in this series of condemnations. How well do you think people remembered his warnings as they went about their daily lives?

THE THEATER OF JESUS' DAY

Herod the Great popularized the theater in Israel. The plays often focused on gods and goddesses, mocked honorable and sacred things, and were bawdy and obscene. Featured actors "painted" their faces to portray different characters or emotions, and leading actors were announced with trumpets. The Greek word for "stage actor" was *hypocrite*.

The Jewish community considered theaters to be immoral, and the Talmud taught that no one should attend them. There is no evidence that Jesus participated in or attended the theater, but he clearly was familiar with this aspect of his culture. He used the images of stage actors to warn people against impure motives—performing their acts of righteousness before men rather than doing them out of a sincere desire to please God (Matthew 6:1–18). By speaking the "language" of the theater, Jesus could communicate to those who knew the theater, including the pagans of the Decapolis.

THEATER AT SEPPHORIS

WORTH OBSERVING
Jesus and the Pharisees

We must remember that while Jesus exposed and criticized some of the Pharisees, not all of them were hypocrites. Many were a powerful force for good among Jesus' people and had a theology similar to that which the early Christians developed. Some of them were not far from God's kingdom (Mark 12:34). Some supported Jesus' ministry and invited him to their homes (Luke 7:36; 14:1); others tried to protect him (John 3:1–2; 7:50–51; Luke 13:31). Some Pharisees, in fact, became followers of Jesus (Acts 15:5) and kept teaching other people (Acts 23:6; Philippians 3:4–6).

Note the following beliefs that the Pharisees had in common with Jesus:

- The physical resurrection of the dead
- A coming judgment day followed by reward or punishment
- Expectation of the Messiah's return
- Belief in angels
- Recognition of a combination of free choice and divine control in human life
- That God was all-wise, all-knowing, just, merciful, and loving
- The importance of completely obeying God's law
- People's power to choose good or evil, using the Torah as their guide

Despite these similarities, Jesus did have conflicts with some Pharisees. Although many Pharisees set high moral standards and tried to remain devoted to God in a hostile world without resorting to the Zealots' violence, others were not godly and righteous. Some were so zealous concerning interpretations of oral law that they violated the very letter of the Torah. Other Pharisees focused so much on obedience that they didn't notice or care about people's needs.

Unfortunately, history perceives Pharisees as hypocrites—stubborn, uncaring, religious fanatics who rejected and hated Jesus and sought his arrest and conviction. Jesus, however, understood their thinking and often tailored his message to make sure they would understand it. So it is important to realize that Jesus never criticized anyone for *being* a Pharisee. Rather, he criticized their hypocrisy—the fact that they knew the truth but didn't live by it. Jesus commanded his followers to obey the Pharisees (Matthew 23:2–7) but not to imitate their hypocrisy.

Reflection

Theaters played a key role in disseminating the Hellenistic world-view during the first century. Godly Jews resisted their allure and sought to remain focused on God and his Word. In a similar way, followers of Jesus today must use the same diligence to hold onto the values of Jesus rather than giving in to secular humanism. We each must decide which aspects of culture to participate in and which to avoid. But even as we do this, we must remember that Jesus also knew enough about the theater and other prominent aspects of culture to use them as teaching illustrations.

As Christians, we often struggle to be distinctive in a secular world. What have you learned from Jesus' example about speaking in a "language" (words, methods, media) that our culture speaks so that our message can be understood?

Hellenistic theaters promoted a worldview quite different from a biblical worldview, so godly Jews did not attend the theater.

What in your culture would correspond to the theater of Jesus' day?

Which popular aspects of culture promote worldviews opposite from a biblical worldview?

What criteria do you use to determine which aspects of culture to participate in (and be aware of) and which ones to avoid entirely?

When Christians choose not to participate in certain events, but criticize those events without knowing much about them, what message(s) are they sending to people who do participate in them?

What message do Christians send when they can talk knowledgeably about their culture and even use it to help communicate Jesus' message?

FOR FURTHER STUDY

The book *Roaring Lambs: A Gentle Plan to Radically Change Your World* by Robert Briner (Zondervan, 1993) makes a powerful case for learning to speak to a desperate culture in ways it understands. It includes many examples and recommendations.

DATA FILE
Herod and the Theater

More than any other person, Herod the Great was responsible for bringing the theater to Israel. His campaign to make humanistic Hellenism the world-view of his people included building theaters at Caesarea, Jericho, Jerusalem, Samaria, and Sidon. Many other places including Susita, Sepphoris, the Decapolis, and Beth Shan had theaters as well. Certainly the first-century theater, which often opposed the God-centered worldview of the Jews, was an important influence in the culture.

The splendor and size of Hellenistic theaters, such as the one in Sepphoris, were seductive and overwhelming to the Jewish people. Imagine living in a small village such as Nazareth with a few hundred people and then having the opportunity to see sensual plays in a beautiful theater that could hold thousands of spectators. The religious community, realizing the pull of the theater, resisted it strongly. An ancient rabbi named Yitzak is quoted in the *Megilla*, a collection of Jewish sayings, as believing that Caesarea and Jerusalem could not prosper at the same time. Either one or the other would be in ruins. He clearly understood that the values represented by Caesarea and its theater were antithetical to those of Jerusalem and God's temple.

THEATER AT CAESAREA

Day Three | Jesus the Master Builder

The Very Words of God

> He [Christ] is *"the stone you builders rejected, which has become the capstone." Salvation is found in no one else, for there is no other name under heaven given to men by which we must be saved.*
>
> **Acts 4:11 – 12**

Bible Discovery

Jesus Builds His Church

Jesus was a trained *tekton,* a builder, in a land where there was lots of rock and very little wood. Although he would have known how to build out of wood, he probably spent most of his time working as a stonemason, shaping and laying stones. So it was quite natural for Jesus to use images from the construction world — from the buildings his audiences saw every day of their lives — in his teaching.

1. On what did Jesus say he would build his church, and what did that image convey to his audience? (See Matthew 16:18.)

   NOTE: Although there are different interpretations as to precisely what Jesus intended the "rock" to mean, two major viewpoints are: Jesus' identity as the Messiah and the faith of his disciples as represented by Peter.

2. After seeing the spectacular construction of Herod's temple, what claim did Jesus make, and what impact did it have on the people who heard him? (See John 2:19 – 22.)

3. When addressing his disciples about their commitment to follow him, Jesus drew an analogy between building a tower and becoming his disciple. What was his point? (See Luke 14:28–30.)

4. With which part of a building did Jesus identify himself, and why do you think he used this metaphor to describe his role? (See Matthew 21:42; Acts 4:11–12.)

5. Following Jesus' example, Peter also used images of stone construction to explain what it means to participate in the kingdom of God. (See 1 Peter 2:4–8.)

   a. Who (or what) is Jesus in Peter's analogy?

   b. What is Jesus the *tekton* building today, and with whom?

   c. What is Jesus to those who reject him and why?

Reflection

Today Jesus, the precious cornerstone of his church, still holds everything together. Yet, many people discount him and what he accomplished on earth. They reject him and refuse to acknowledge that salvation can come only through him.

Picture for a moment the buildings in the world in which Jesus taught — the simple stone houses of rural villages, the enormous cut stones of Herod's temple in Jerusalem, the magnificent carved pillars and walls of Roman-style palaces and theaters.

What do you think people of Jesus' day thought of when Jesus spoke of himself as the cornerstone of his church?

What do you think people thought about themselves and their role in God's kingdom when Peter spoke of believers as being living stones in God's house?

With these images of Israel's stone buildings in mind, how do you think differently about yourself and your walk with God? About your understanding of what the church is called to be?

Peter wrote that God's people are being built into a "holy priesthood" (1 Peter 2:9 – 10). How willing are you to allow Jesus the *tekton,* the master builder, to shape you into the person he desires you to be?

How willing are you to pay the cost of being a disciple of Jesus?

How much of an honor is it for a follower of Jesus to be a living stone in the "spiritual house" God is building?

Many people today struggle with the message of Acts 4:12 because they want to believe that all religions are the same and that any belief is fine as long as it "works" for people. Why can't another "stone" replace Jesus and fill his role?

Memorize

> *But each one should be careful how he builds. For no one can lay any foundation other than the one already laid, which is Jesus Christ.*
>
> *1 Corinthians 3:10 – 11*

Day Four | The Significance of Nazareth

The Very Words of God

> *When he [Joseph] heard that Archelaus was reigning in Judea in place of his father Herod, he was afraid to go there. Having been warned in a dream, he withdrew to the district of Galilee, and he went and lived in a town called Nazareth. So was fulfilled what was said through the prophets: "He will be called a Nazarene."*
>
> *Matthew 2:22 – 23*

Bible Discovery

Jesus the Nazarene

Joseph and Mary originally made their home in the small village of Nazareth in Lower Galilee. At the time of Jesus' birth, however, they were in Bethlehem for the census required by Caesar Augustus. When King Herod sought to kill the infant Jesus, an angel warned Joseph and the family fled to Egypt, where they remained until Herod died. An angel told Joseph when it was time to return to Israel, and as it turns out, where they chose to live was an important part of who Jesus was.

1. When Joseph brought Mary and Jesus back to Israel, where did they settle and why does this matter? (See Matthew 2:21 – 23.)

2. How was Jesus identified by the people of his day, and how widespread was this knowledge? (See Mark 14:67; 16:6; Luke 4:34; 18:37; John 1:45.)

3. Although there is no record of a prophet specifically saying, "He will be called a Nazarene," Jesus' identity as a Nazarene did fulfill the ancient prophecies. In order to understand this, we must understand the meaning of the word *Nazareth*. The Greek word translated Nazareth (or Nazarene) is most likely derived from the Hebrew word *netzer*, which means "shoot" or "branch." This word is frequently used to refer to the royal line of David.

    Read the following Scripture passages and note the expressions the prophets used to describe the Messiah:

Scripture Text	Expression Related to the Messiah
Isaiah 11:1 – 2, 10	
Isaiah 53:2	

Jeremiah 23:5	
Jeremiah 33:15	
Zechariah 3:8	
Zechariah 6:12	

4. Can you see the connection between the Davidic branch and Nazareth? The description "Jesus the Nazarene," meaning "Jesus the Branch," linked Jesus to the prophecies stating that the Messiah would be the branch that would grow out of Jesse's stump. What did Jesus say about himself to confirm this identity? (See Revelation 22:16.)

5. Based on their name and Davidic lineage, the Nazarenes believed that the Messiah would come from their village because they were the "shoot" village.

   a. What does Luke 4:16 – 30 tell us about what the Nazarenes thought of themselves?

   b. What did other people think of Nazareth? (See John 1:45 – 46.)

Reflection

Although they were not highly regarded by other Galileans, the residents of Nazareth — "Nazarenes" — passionately believed the Scriptures. They treasured the Word of God and took seriously the prophecies concerning the lineage of David and the Messiah. They looked forward to the coming of the Messiah. Imagine the faith it took to believe this in the face of criticism from other Jews and the insignificant appearance and size of their village. No wonder they were outraged when Jesus said Isaiah's prophecy about the Messiah was being fulfilled and then said, "No prophet is accepted in his hometown" (Luke 4:16 – 24)!

What do you think enabled the people of Nazareth to keep trusting in God to fulfill the prophecies concerning the Messiah?

How easy or difficult do you think it was for them to do this?

How might your life be different if you chose, as the people of Nazareth did, to trust completely in God's promises despite improbable circumstances?

What would help you do this? How well, for example do you know the Scriptures? How often during your day do you meditate on the Scriptures? How often do you think about what you have read and consider it in light of your circumstances and future?

Knowing the Scriptures, Jesus chose to be identified as Jesus of Nazareth. On what have you chosen to base your identity, and what difference does it make in your life?

Day Five | Jesus: The "Shoot" from Jesse's Stump

The Very Words of God

> *A shoot will come up from the stump of Jesse; from his roots a Branch will bear fruit. The Spirit of the LORD will rest on him — the Spirit of wisdom and of understanding, the Spirit of counsel and of power, the Spirit of knowledge and of the fear of the LORD.*
>
> Isaiah 11:1 – 2

Bible Discovery

The Image of the Olive Tree

When olive trees grow old, their branches no longer produce fruit, so the farmer will cut off those branches, leaving a stump several feet tall. Soon, new shoots begin to grow out of the old stump, or new branches are sometimes grafted onto the old stump. From this new growth, the tree will once again produce an abundant crop of olives. The prophets, Jesus, and the apostle Paul used the image of this enduring quality of the olive tree, which was familiar to the people of Jesus' day, to help explain his messianic task and relationship to his people.

THE METAPHOR OF THE OLIVE TREE AND ITS BRANCHES

- The roots and stump represent Israel.
- The faces in the stump are renderings of Abraham and Sarah, parents of the Jewish people.
- The large branches represent Jesus, the shoot or branch of Jesse.
- The smaller branches represent those who believe in the Messiah.

THE OLIVE TREE

1. In order to understand the metaphor of the olive tree, we must know what it represents. What is the identity of the "stump" and the "shoot"? (See Isaiah 11:1 – 3; 53:1 – 5.)

DID YOU KNOW?

The title given to Jesus — *Christ* (from the Greek) and *Messiah* (from the Hebrew) — means "anointed." It occurs more than 375 times in the New Testament. This title is related to the olive tree because Old Testament priests and kings were anointed with oil, most likely olive oil (Exodus 29:7; 1 Samuel 16:13). This is one more way the olive tree, which produces precious oil, is a metaphor for the Messiah, God's anointed priest and king.

2. In John 15:1, Jesus uses the metaphor of the vine and branches as another way to identify himself as the "stump" or "tree." Note what Jesus reveals about God's relationship to the tree:

    a. What must God, the gardener, do to a tree that will not produce good fruit? (See Matthew 3:8 – 10; 7:17 – 19.)

    b. When has God had to do this, and what was the result? (See Isaiah 6:11 – 13.)

3. What were early Christians called (Acts 24:5), and what did that description mean (Jeremiah 33:15)? Remember, *netzer,* the root of Nazareth, means "branch" or "shoot."

4. Romans 11:13 – 24 describes the relationship between Jesus the Nazarene, the Jewish people, and Gentile Christians. Fill in the following blanks:

    a. Gentile Christians are not "natural" branches of the stump. They are _____ that have been _____ among the others. (See Romans 11:17.)

    b. Gentile Christians share in the _____
from the olive root and must remember that they do
not _____ the root, but in fact receive
_____ the root. (See Romans 11:17 – 18.)

5. Gentile Christians are expected to produce fruit just as Israel
was expected to produce fruit.

    a. What enables the branches to produce fruit? (See John
15:4 – 5.)

    b. What will happen to branches that do not produce fruit?
(See John 15:6; Romans 11:21 – 22.)

Reflection

If you have chosen to follow Jesus, you will face great challenges.
The evil one will do everything he can to sidetrack you, to try to
separate you from the life-giving presence and power of Jesus, "the
true vine." The evil one will tempt you to try to live life in your own
strength and distract you from your task of bearing good fruit.

Drawing on the image of the Nazarenes being "people of the
branch," would you say that you are a branch that has been
grafted onto the stump? Why or why not?

Are you a branch that is grafted strongly into the stump, or is
your life-giving "connection" to Jesus a bit weak?

In what way(s) does Jesus' statement, "Apart from me you can do nothing," collide with the belief of our culture that considers independent, personal success to be the greatest accomplishment?

To what extent do you depend on the "stump" for nourishment, and in what ways do you seek "nourishment" from other sources?

If you are a disciple of Jesus, a branch on God's tree, why is bearing fruit to be a necessary part of your life?

How deep is your commitment to producing good fruit?

Which specific area of your life is unfruitful, or at least not producing the kind of fruit it should produce?

Are you willing to cut away what is not fruitful, or are you waiting for the "gardener" to do it?

The metaphor of the olive tree communicated clearly to the people of Jesus' time, but for most Christians today it is a new image and a foreign concept. In what ways has this study of the olive tree and the vine and branches helped you better understand your faith? What Jesus has done for you? Your Jewish roots as a "branch" grafted onto the "stump"? Your calling and task in God's kingdom?

Memorize

I am the true vine, and my Father is the gardener. He cuts off every branch in me that bears no fruit, while every branch that does bear fruit he prunes so that it will be even more fruitful. You are already clean because of the word I have spoken to you. Remain in me, and I will remain in you. No branch can bear fruit by itself; it must remain in the vine. Neither can you bear fruit unless you remain in me. I am the vine; you are the branches. If a man remains in me and I in him, he will bear much fruit; apart from me you can do nothing.

John 15:1 – 5

DATA FILE
The Pharisees
Their History

When the Maccabees opposed the Greeks in 167 BC, they were supported by a group of pious Jews called the Hasidim. These mighty warriors, who were also Torah teachers and scholars, were devoted to God and sought to obey him in everything they did. But eventually even the Jewish leaders (descendants of the Maccabees) became as Hellenistic as the Greeks. When that happened, the devout Jews believed they had no choice but to separate themselves from the Jewish leaders in Jerusalem.

Some of these Jewish separatists became Zealots who chose to battle the influence of paganism violently—among their fellow Jews as well as the Romans. Another group of separatists decided that violence would not work. They believed that God had allowed (even caused) the foreign oppression because his people had failed to obey the Torah. Therefore, they believed that people should devote themselves to obeying every detail of the law and separate themselves from all influences that might interfere with their devotion. These separatists took the name *perushim* (meaning "separate" or "separatists"), which translated to English is "Pharisee." Committed totally to God, they assumed the responsibility of leading Israel back to him. By the time of Jesus, there were more than 6,000 Pharisees.

Their Beliefs

The Torah was the focus of the Pharisees' lives. They believed that Moses had given a two-part law: the written law of Torah and additional oral commandments that had been passed from generation to generation to help the faithful understand and apply the written law. The Pharisees continued to interpret and expand the Torah to cover every possible occurrence of unfaithfulness to the written law. As you might expect, this oral law became a complex guide to everyday life—far more complicated than most people could understand. In fact, the Pharisees' "yoke" of Torah—the method of obedience—was so difficult to understand that it sometimes obscured the very law they sought to obey.

continued on next page . . .

The Pharisees differed significantly from the Sadducees, another group of religious Jewish leaders with whom Jesus communicated. Notice the contrasts:

Pharisees	Sadducees
Committed to studying and obeying the Torah and oral law	Controlled the economy of the temple in Jerusalem; faithful to temple rituals but often Hellenistic in lifestyle; dealt harshly with anyone who undermined the temple, its economy, or its ritual
Had a minor role in the Sanhedrin — the ruling religious council used by the Herods and Romans as the instrument to govern the Jewish people	Had a majority in the Sanhedrin — the ruling religious council — though some scholars believe there were fewer than 1,000 of them
Believed in the Torah and oral law	Believed in the written Torah and rejected oral law; opposed the Pharisees until the temple was destroyed in AD 70; believed study of Torah undermined temple ritual
Believed in bodily resurrection and angels	Rejected belief in bodily resurrection as well as most Pharisaical doctrine concerning angels and spirits
Gained authority based on piety and knowledge	Gained authority through position and birth
Worshiped in the synagogue	Believed synagogue worship undermined temple ritual and the economy of the temple (their income)
As a whole, were not intimidated by Jesus	Feared and hated Jesus, whose popularity they feared would undermine their position in the Sanhedrin and Rome's support

MISGUIDED FAITH

The history of those who have sought to follow God is marked by situations in which God's people lost sight of God's way of doing things and chose to follow their own ways. Examples of this tendency from the era we have been studying include Pharisees who believed that only single-minded dedication to the Torah would please God, Zealots who tried to bring about God's kingdom through violence, and Essenes who called for isolation and separation from the world. In this session, we will consider another example of God's people losing sight of God's way — the great tragedy of Christianity, the Crusades. We will contrast Jesus' teachings with that terrible invasion of the Holy Land by European Crusaders beginning in the eleventh century.

Our video begins at the ruins of a Crusader fort named Belvoir that stands high above the Jordan Valley. Here fifty knights, about 450 soldiers, and their families and staff lived. The fort's beautiful and seemingly peaceful location gives little indication of the horror it represents.

Instead of demonstrating the love, compassion, forgiveness, and self-sacrifice that Jesus used to communicate his message, some Crusaders decided that all people who did not belong to their tradition of Christianity should no longer live. So, as they left Europe to liberate the Holy Land from the "infidels," these Crusaders slaughtered innocent inhabitants of cities, towns, and villages. Entire Jewish communities were locked in their synagogues and burned to death. Towns were plundered because their inhabitants were Jewish or Muslim in ethnic or religious background. As they entered Turkey, Crusaders slaughtered more "infidels," some of whom were actually orthodox Christians — brothers and sisters in the faith who simply looked like Muslims. Crusaders did this with the full support of popes and other religious leaders.

For nearly 200 years, under the sign of the cross and in Jesus' name, Crusaders used violence and hatred as a means of presenting the gospel of peace. Their overall actions were inconsistent with Jesus' commands and defamed his name. Although the Crusades caused the gospel to spread to new areas (primarily by clergy who came after the Crusades), the movement as a whole greatly damaged Christianity's reputation. It turned many Jews and Muslims away from God. Even today, the Crusades strongly influence people's perceptions of Christianity in the Middle East. They stand as a wall between Christians and people of other faiths.

The Crusades comprise a sad chapter in Christian history. These "holy wars" illustrate how easily Christians justify methods and atti-tudes other than those that Jesus commanded and lived out. How can Christians today tell people about Jesus' message of love when the ruins of fortresses and battlements built by Christians who came to destroy and kill still occupy the hilltops? We must be careful to demonstrate Jesus as he proclaimed himself to be — Savior, not war-rior. We must model our attitudes and behavior after his so that we can truly reflect him to a spiritually dark, hurting world.

Just as God called the Jews of the Old Testament to live at the world's crossroads and demonstrate the character of the living God to a watching, spiritually hungry world, Jesus calls his disciples to do the same. We are called to use Jesus' methods of love, kindness, forgiveness, and self-sacrifice to show other people God's character and the wonder of a personal relationship with him.

Therefore, we must be as committed to the methods of Jesus as we are to the salvation message he died to provide. We must always confront evil, but never for our own gain. We do it because we are involved in our culture and are concerned for those around us who do not know him. Jesus' message is desperately needed in our world. God gave it to us as a treasure to give away, not to hoard in isolated fortresses.

Opening Thoughts (4 minutes)

The Very Words of God

> Be imitators of God, therefore, as dearly loved children and live a life of love, just as Christ loved us and gave himself up for us as a fragrant offering and sacrifice to God.
>
> Ephesians 5:1 – 2

Think About It

We all know people who have rejected Jesus and the gift of salvation he freely offers. Think for a moment about the people you know who have rejected God because of the poor example of Christians.

What turned these people away? What might have drawn them toward him? It may help you to think about the people who influenced your discovery of God and what they did that drew you toward him.

DVD Teaching Notes (13 minutes)

The Crusaders' fort

The Crusaders' actions and motivation

The damaging consequences of the Crusaders

Our response: choosing Jesus' message and his methods

DVD Discussion (8 minutes)

Look at the map on page 233. Note how far the Crusaders had to travel to get to the Holy Land. Try to imagine the killing and pillaging that took place all along their route. It's nearly impossible to comprehend what was done in Jesus' name, isn't it?

1. What have you learned about the Crusades that you did not know before, and in what ways has your perception of the Crusades changed as a result?

2. What kind of an impression did the European-style Crusader fort high above the Jordan Valley leave with you? What kind of an impression do you think it makes on Jews and Muslims who live in Israel and Jordan today?

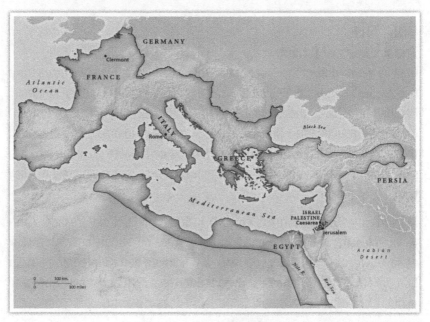

THE WORLD OF THE CRUSADERS

3. What happens to people's view of Christianity when those who are supposed to be imitating Jesus choose their own methods of interacting with the world?

4. What things do Christians do today (perhaps unknowingly) in terms of language as well as action that to some people are negative reminders of the Crusades?

DATA FILE
The Fortress of Belvoir

Built by the Knights of the Order of the Hospitalers during the twelfth century, this isolated fortress protected the eastern side of the Crusaders' kingdom. Perched on a hill of the Issachar Plateau 1,700 feet above the Jordan Valley, the fortress enabled Crusaders to control the road below and to protect themselves from the local population. From their isolated position, the Crusaders were unable to exert any daily influence on people living in the valley below.

Muslims attacked the fortress from AD 1180–1184, but the Crusaders prevailed. Muslims besieged it again in 1187. After resisting sieges for a total of seven years, the fifty knights and 450 soldiers surrendered and left for Europe. The Muslims then destroyed the fortress so it could never be used again.

Today, the ruins of Belvoir stand as a grim monument to the tragedies that occur when people misunderstand Jesus' message and do not live by the truths he taught. Only by living *in* our culture and confronting evil as

BELVOIR

it presents itself in daily life are we able to influence culture positively for Jesus. He called his people to be community builders, not fortress builders. He called his people to confront evil with the "weapons" of love, compassion, forgiveness, and self-sacrifice.

Physical Details of the Fortress

- A moat encircled the fortress on three sides.
- The entrance was on the east side.
- Towers stood in each corner and in the center of the outer walls so archers could be closer to attackers. A huge tower defended the gate area.
- Small gates led from each tower into the moat, so knights could attack anyone trying to undermine the walls.
- Inside the outer walls (made of basalt) was a smaller fortress consisting of four vaulted, two-story walls and a courtyard. Upper-story rooms were decorated with frescoed plaster.
- Cisterns were dug beneath the vaulted rooms.
- A church made of limestone provided a place for worship on the second floor.

Small Group Bible Discovery and Discussion (23 minutes)

Confronting Evil Jesus' Way

Make no mistake: Jesus confronted evil. He not only confronted it, he sent his followers out to confront it as well. Our human tendency is to confront evil with anger, violence, and revenge, but Jesus confronted evil in a different way. He battled evil through the power of love, kindness, compassion, forgiveness, and self-sacrifice.

1. When Jesus was in the region of Tyre and Sidon, he healed a Canaanite woman's daughter who was possessed by a demon. (See Matthew 15:21 – 28.)

a. What was the longstanding reputation of that area, and how do you think most religious Jews would have viewed it? (See 1 Kings 16:30 – 32; Isaiah 23:17.)

b. Why do you think Jesus went there? (See Matthew 9:10 – 13.)

2. In the following Scripture passages, what did Jesus confront and what can we learn from his methods, attitudes, and actions?

Matthew 16:21 – 25

Mark 5:1 – 20

3. In Luke 10:1 – 3 and 17 – 20, what did Jesus send his followers out into the world to do, and what was the result?

What do you learn from this experience about the inherent confrontation that takes place when followers of Jesus share the message of the kingdom of God?

FACTS TO CONSIDER
As They Saw It

Many people who lived during Jesus' time offered their own solutions to the problems of the day, as the following chart reveals:

Who Had a Solution?	What Was Their Method?	What Was Jesus' Method?
The Pharisees	National obedience to the Torah as a life commitment and the means to bring God's blessing	Demonstrated his commitment to God by his obedience to the Torah
The Essenes	Be separate from the world and wait for God to act	Had a similar theology, yet surrounded himself with people he loved and to whom he ministered
The Zealots	Violence is necessary to bring about God's kingdom in Israel; it was their duty to throw off the chains of Roman rule by every means possible	Taught his disciples to love their enemies
The Herodians and Sadducees	Preached cooperation with Rome; sought to maintain the status quo; were willing to compromise God's law	Was unwilling to compromise God's law in order to keep an earthly peace

4. In his Sermon on the Mount, Jesus outlined his battle plan for confronting evil.

   a. Which characteristics of confrontation did Jesus call "blessed"? (See Matthew 5:3 – 11.)

   b. What is the purpose of following Jesus' battle plan? (See Matthew 5:13 – 16.)

c. In what ways do these characteristics and purposes differ from the Crusaders' ways of confronting evil? Our ways of confronting evil?

Faith Lesson (6 minutes)

Wherever Jesus went to share the message of the kingdom of God, he encountered evil. Sometimes evil presented itself as opposition from those who rejected his teaching. Sometimes it hid in the suffering of a demon-possessed child or a crippled man. Sometimes it was revealed through the words of his own disciples. And sometimes evil was expressed in unbelief. In every instance, Jesus defeated it with love, compassion, forgiveness, and self-sacrifice.

Just as Jesus confronted evil in ways quite different from most people in his culture, Christians today are called to respond in ways that reflect his heart and his methods. Consider what might happen if you, and other Christians, were to consistently take the message of the kingdom of God into the world and confront evil in the ways Jesus did.

1. As you have tried to follow Jesus and communicate the message of his kingdom to other people, to what extent have you been aware of your role in confronting evil?

2. When you have faced a confrontation with evil, how have you responded?

As other people have observed your actions and attitudes, what have they seen of Jesus? What have they seen of someone or something else?

Rather than using the motivations, attitudes, and/or methods that Jesus used, which of your own have you sometimes used in confronting evil?

In what ways have you harmed Jesus' reputation by not using his methods of love, compassion, kindness, forgiveness, and self-sacrifice?

3. In our world, which do you think shines brighter and makes a greater impact when it is used against evil — violence and payback or forgiveness and love?

What one change will you make from living your way to living Jesus' way so that the light of Christ will shine brightly in your life as you confront evil in your world?

Closing (1 minute)

Read Romans 12:17 – 19 together: "Do not repay anyone evil for evil. Be careful to do what is right in the eyes of everybody. If it is possible, as far as it depends on you, live at peace with everyone. Do not take revenge, my friends, but leave room for God's wrath, for it is written: 'It is mine to avenge; I will repay,' says the Lord." Then pray, asking God's forgiveness for the times you have chosen to live your way rather than his way. Ask God to forgive the times you have given people the wrong idea of Jesus and created barriers to their knowledge and acceptance of him. Ask God to empower you to live faithfully according to Jesus' teaching, to truly walk in his light so that you may guide people toward Jesus.

Memorize

Do not repay anyone evil for evil. Be careful to do what is right in the eyes of everybody. If it is possible, as far as it depends on you, live at peace with everyone. Do not take revenge, my friends, but leave room for God's wrath, for it is written: "It is mine to avenge; I will repay," says the Lord.

Romans 12:17 – 19

Understanding the World in Which Jesus Lived

In-Depth Personal Study Sessions

Day One | Jesus Issues the Commands of God's Kingdom

The Very Words of God

> *I tell you who hear me: Love your enemies, do good to those who hate you, bless those who curse you, pray for those who mistreat you. If someone strikes you on one cheek, turn to him the other also. If someone takes your cloak, do not stop him from taking your tunic. Give to everyone who asks you, and if anyone takes what belongs to you, do not demand it back. Do to others as you would have them do to you.*
>
> *Luke 6:27–31*

Bible Discovery

Do Everything in Love

In everything he did, Jesus displayed God's love. He loved us so much that he gave himself as the sacrifice for the sins of the world. Instead of destroying all the opposition he encountered, Jesus reached out in love to meet people's needs. As disciples of Jesus, we also have the opportunity to live in the light of his kingdom and demonstrate Jesus' love to hurting people. But living in love rarely comes easily for us. To help in this endeavor, consider some of the instructions Jesus gave his disciples about how to live in love.

1. What command did Jesus give during the Last Supper to all who would be his disciples? Why is it important? (See John 13:34–35.)

2. Instead of advocating violent, self-serving ways to change the world, Jesus chose the way of love. If we are his followers, living in love is essential for us as well. Consider each of the following commands of Jesus on how to live in love, then write down what it would look like for you to live them out in your world.

Jesus' Commands	Living Them Out in My World
Matt. 5:5–7	
Matt. 5:8	
Matt. 5:9	
Matt. 5:13–16	
Matt. 5:23–24	
Matt. 5:38–42	
Matt. 5:43–48	
Matt. 6:14–15	

Reflection

Some of the commands Jesus gave his followers are challenging for us — they are the opposite of how we are inclined to respond. Yet God calls us to be Jesus' hands and feet and to change our world by living in love. In order to accomplish this, each of us must learn how to live in and interact with our culture with the same spirit of love that Jesus modeled for us. We must pay close attention to the person we are becoming to discern whether or not we are living more by Jesus' commands or by our own agendas.

When have you seen followers of Jesus truly love people through the Spirit that lives within them?

What have you seen the love of Jesus, as demonstrated by his followers, accomplish in your life or in the lives of others?

What message about the kingdom of God have these demonstrations of love conveyed to you, to others?

In what ways have these examples of love encouraged you to change how you interact with other people?

If loving as Jesus loved is the litmus test for true discipleship, would it be accurate to describe yourself as a true disciple of Jesus? Why or why not?

If you truly want to be known in your world as a disciple of Jesus who loves as he loves, which character qualities and behaviors of love do you need to pursue?

How quickly, for example, do you seek reconciliation when disagreement arises with a coworker, a family member, or another believer?

How earnestly, for example, do you pray for those who seek to harm you?

How readily, for example, do you forgive those who wrong you?

Memorize

You have heard that it was said, "Love your neighbor and hate your enemy." But I tell you: Love your enemies and pray for those who persecute you.

Matthew 5:43 – 44

PROFILE OF A MOVEMENT
Soldiers of the Cross

On November 27, 1095, in Clermont, France, Pope Urban II called upon all true Christians to free the Holy Land from what he considered to be Muslim infidels. Christian pilgrims were unable to visit holy sites, including the Church of the Holy Sepulchre. That speech sparked violent conflict between European Christians and Muslims of the Middle East. Thousands of knights, serfs, peasants, and even a few kings sewed the sign of the cross on the front of their tunics and went to war for Jesus Christ. The Jews, without a country, were caught in the conflict.

The First Crusade

Setting out from Clermont, France, knights, farmers, shopkeepers, and fortune seekers headed east through Germany and then south and east to the Holy Land. Determined to avenge Jesus' crucifixion in blood, they massacred many Jews living in wealthy communities in Germany. Many other Jews committed suicide as the knights and unruly mob entered their towns. Tens of thousands of Muslims were also killed. Crusaders continued to slaughter innocent people, even Orthodox Christians who had the misfortune of looking like Muslims.

Finally the Crusaders reached Jerusalem, which they captured on July 15, 1099. A terrible massacre ensued; streets were awash with the blood of innocent civilians. The Jews and Muslims who survived were sold into slavery, and Christianity had earned a reputation that would last for millennia.

The knights built great, European-style castles on high hills, far from roads and sometimes far from water. Soon the castles became places of refuge, escape, and even prisons. Having traveled thousands of miles to win the Holy Land and expose the "infidels" to God's truth, the European conquerors had no gospel to offer their subjects. They lived in isolation, not influencing the day-to-day lives of the common people. Jesus would not have recognized these soldiers who came to spread his kingdom because they knew so little about the methods he had taught and the way of sacrifice he had walked.

continued on next page . . .

The Second Crusade

In 1144, an itinerant monk began urging soldiers to destroy the Jewish communities of Germany to avenge Jesus' crucifixion. As a result, many more innocent people were slaughtered in Jesus' name.

The Third Crusade

Spared the horrors of the first two Crusades, Jewish communities in England were not as fortunate in 1170. During this Crusade, Jews in York, Lynn, Norwich, Stamford, and other towns were massacred. Thus England, too, joined the roster of countries whose "Christian" armies distinguished themselves in their brutality against "infidels."

The Fourth Crusade

In 1198, Pope Innocent III ordered Jews to wear badges to identify themselves. He then ordered them to be killed to atone for Jesus' death.

The Shepherds' Crusade

The Crusades formally ended in 1291 when Muslims recaptured the Holy Land. But a few years later, European Jews were subjected to yet another Crusade. Nearly 40,000, mostly teenage "Crusaders" pillaged, killed, and burned their way across Europe. Some sources indicate that these "soldiers of the cross" exterminated 150 communities of Jews.

Day Two | A Disciple Learns from Jesus' Example

The Very Words of God

> *Therefore, since Christ suffered in his body, arm yourselves also with the same attitude, because he who has suffered in his body is done with sin. As a result, he does not live the rest of his earthly life for evil human desires, but rather for the will of God.*

1 Peter 4:1 – 2

Bible Discovery

Peter Learns to Confront Evil in a New Way

A disciple of Jesus seeks to live the way he lived, to become like him in every way. So when it comes to confronting evil, it's important to know what Jesus taught and to dedicate ourselves to following his example. Then we can begin to confront immorality, injustice, selfishness, greed, and other forms of evil in ways that represent his will and model his attitudes and behavior.

1. Peter was one of the disciples at Jesus' side the night he was arrested. How did Peter respond when the armed soldiers and officials from the chief priests and Pharisees came to the garden of Gethsemane? (See John 18:1 – 5, 8 – 11.)

   How do we know that this was not how Jesus wanted Peter to confront the evil they faced that night?

   What greater evil was Jesus confronting that night? How was he going to do it? What was his attitude toward what he faced?

2. No doubt Peter never forgot the events of the night Jesus was arrested. It appears that night initiated a dramatic change in Peter's approach to confronting evil. What differences do you see in Peter's attitude toward evil and methods

for confronting evil in 1 Peter 3:8–17 as opposed to what he evidently thought and did in the garden of Gethsemane?

How is such a change possible?

Which principles did Peter set forth to guide us in confronting evil?

What kind of blessings will people who put these principles into action receive?

What does Peter's statement, "Always be prepared to give an answer to everyone who asks you to give the reason for the hope that you have," have to do with confronting evil? Why do you think it was important for Peter to say this?

3. As Peter described how to live in a way that sets apart Jesus as Lord, he warned that sometimes we will suffer for doing what is right and good. (See 1 Peter 3:13–17.) What did Jesus say his followers could expect as they went out to share his

message and confront evil in his name, and what encouragement did he offer? (See Matthew 10:17 – 28.)

Reflection

When we confront evil using methods other than those Jesus used and taught, we send the wrong message about the kingdom of God, and we defame Jesus' reputation. Jesus certainly wants us to confront the evil in our culture, but he wants us to do it as he did — not by wielding the sword, but by offering his life.

To which of your actions in confronting evil would Jesus say, "Put your _____ away"?

What alternative course of action would Jesus want you to take?

Chances are you will meet someone whose view of Christianity has been affected negatively by tragedies such as the Crusades or another kind of wrong treatment by Christians.

What do you think Jesus would do or say to reach out to that person?

In what practical ways might you reach out to such a person and demonstrate who Jesus truly is? Which actions and words have the power to start undoing the damage that has been done to Jesus' reputation?

Day Three | Live at the Crossroads of Your Culture

The Very Words of God

You are the light of the world. A city on a hill cannot be hidden. Neither do people light a lamp and put it under a bowl. Instead they put it on its stand, and it gives light to everyone in the house. In the same way, let your light shine before men, that they may see your good deeds and praise your Father in heaven.

Matthew 5:14 – 16

Bible Discovery

Let the Light of Jesus Shine in Your World

The Crusaders abandoned Jesus' self-sacrificing methods and isolated themselves from culture. They dominated the political scene, yet had little influence on people's daily lives. God, however, calls his people to live at the crossroads of life so that the world will come to know that he is truly God. As modern-day Christians, we must live *in* our culture so that we can demonstrate the gospel of Christ to our world.

1. What did God, through the prophet Isaiah, reveal about what his people are to do? (See Isaiah 43:10 – 12.)

What did Jesus command his disciples (and that includes us) to do? (See Matthew 28:19 – 20.)

In what ways are Jesus' disciples to accomplish this? (See Matthew 5:13 – 16.)

2. Matthew 15:29 – 38 reveals one way in which Jesus demonstrated how to be involved in culture.

   a. What specific things did Jesus do, and why?

   b. What was the impact of his actions on the people?

Reflection

It's one thing to think about God's commands to love other people and thereby reveal his kingdom to a watching world, but it is quite another to put those commands into specific action. Yet that is exactly what Jesus did. Again and again he stepped into the crossroads of his culture to teach his disciples how to put their faith into action. Through his personal example, he demonstrated what it looks like to confront evil and model sincere love.

Jesus gave his followers clear instructions for continuing the mission he had begun. They were to build his church, feed the hungry, clothe the naked, and care for the lonely. They were to be peacemakers and servants, to be salt and light. And that is exactly what we are to be.

Take some time to reflect on the following examples of how Jesus and the apostles revealed the kingdom of God to the people they encountered in their world. Then write down some ways that you can make more of an effort to meet the needs and touch the hearts of people in your world. Consider especially how:

- Open you are to responding to people who come to you
- Eager you are to serve those whom others would turn away
- Far out of your comfort zone you will go to reach a needy person
- Dedicated you are to living out the message of God's kingdom in the crossroads of your world

Matthew 7:28 – 8:3

Mark 10:46 – 52

John 4:4 – 14

Galatians 2:7 – 10

Memorize

If anyone has material possessions and sees his brother in need but has no pity on him, how can the love of God be in him? Dear children, let us not love with words or tongue but with actions and in truth.

1 John 3:17 – 18

Day Four | Be Community Builders, Not Fortress Builders

The Very Words of God

> *Now this is our boast: Our conscience testifies that we have conducted ourselves in the world, and especially in our relations with you, in the holiness and sincerity that are from God. We have done so not according to worldly wisdom, but according to God's grace.*
>
> *2 Corinthians 1:12*

Bible Discovery

Building Bridges by God's Grace

The Crusaders stand as a tragic example of how the Christian community sometimes fails to follow Jesus' methods for revealing the kingdom of God. They lived by the power of the sword rather than by God's grace. They isolated themselves and hid the light of the world in fortresses high above the communities they ruled. Instead of building bridges to invite people into the kingdom of God, they built walls that kept them out.

1. In contrast to how the Crusaders lived, what did the apostle Peter urge his readers to do? (See 1 Peter 2:11 – 12.)

   How would following Peter's advice build bridges between Christians and the world?

2. What conduct formed the foundation of Paul's lifestyle and involvement in culture? (See 2 Corinthians 1:12.)

How would following Paul's advice build bridges between Christians and the world?

3. First Corinthians 9:19 – 23 outlines specific ways in which Paul conducted himself in his culture and built bridges to the world around him. Contrast his example with the conduct of the Crusaders and with your own.

Paul's Conduct	The Crusaders' Conduct	My Conduct
Although he was a free man, he was willing to make himself a slave in order to win others to Christ.		
Although he was free from the law, he was willing to come under the law.		
Although he would not compromise obedience to Jesus, he was willing to adjust his lifestyle in order to relate to others.		
He was willing to become weak in order to win the weak.		
He did everything he could to win people to Jesus.		

Reflection

God calls his people to reflect his light wherever they go — to exhibit love, forgiveness, compassion, and grace in a spiritually dark world. Consider the extent to which families, communities, and even nations will be impacted positively if each one of us seeks, with God's help, to build bridges into our culture so that people see who Jesus is and are drawn into a personal relationship with him.

How relevant do you believe the Christian community is in our world?

What kinds of things do you believe hinder Christians from becoming influential witnesses of God in secular culture?

In what ways have you seen the Christian community build fortresses, destroy bridges, or even bring harm to the world?

What specifically can you do, according to God's grace, to begin building bridges in your world?

To what extent would you say that you and your faith community are isolated or involved in today's culture?

If changes need to be made, what are you willing to do?

Where is the "crossroads" of culture where you, with God's help, can minister effectively and make a significant contribution?

HISTORICAL PROFILE
The Jews: A History of Persecution

Although the New Testament records bitter disagreements over significant beliefs between some Jews (particularly Sadducees and certain groups of Pharisees) and the early Christians, there were many beliefs on which Jews and Christians were united. The disciples and apostles frequently were invited to teach in Jewish synagogues (although at times they were also expelled from the synagogues). Wherever they went, they talked to Jewish people about following Jesus (Romans 12).

It wasn't until long after New Testament times that Christians began to blame all Jews for rejecting and crucifying Jesus. Church fathers such as Augustine and Justin Martyr taught that Jews were eternally cursed by God. Soon sermons blaming Jews for Jesus' death were preached on the Christian holy days of Good Friday and Easter. (The fact that Jesus went willingly to his death because of the sins of all people was ignored. Little was said, too, about the Roman soldiers who actually crucified Jesus.)

Constantine, the first Christian emperor, passed many anti-Jewish laws. Gregory VII and other popes forbade interaction between Jews and Christians, and barred Jews from holding office. In the view of many Christians, the Jews were God's enemies. In spite of this oppression, Jewish communities survived and flourished, which increased Gentile resentment and led to further abuse of Jews. Forced conversions and baptisms of Jews became increasingly common, and local violence occasionally flared, wiping out entire communities. Absurd rumors, such as the false accusation that Jews stole Christian children in order to use their blood to make unleavened bread for Passover, ran rampant. Consequently, thousands of innocent Jews died at the hands of their "Christian" neighbors.

During the Crusades, the violence against Jews simply expanded to include Muslims. When the Crusades ended, violence didn't end. For hundreds of years Jewish property was routinely seized. During the Inquisition (from the 1100s through the 1500s), entire communities of Jews were brutally tortured and destroyed. Thousands of other Jews were forced to become Christians. Three hundred thousand Jews were expelled from Spain the year Columbus discovered America. In 1298, more than 100,000 Jews were killed in Germany; 2,000 were burned to death in Strasbourg alone. Martin Luther wrote "Against Jews and Their Lies," a strident treatise condemning Jews to the flames of hell forever. Jewish persecution continued in Russia, Poland, Hungary, and the Ukraine. Still Jewish communities flourished. Then came the Holocaust.

Only recently have formal steps been taken to renounce this dark chapter of Christian history. The Second Vatican Council affirmed the Jewish roots of Christianity and repudiated collective Jewish guilt for Jesus' death. The Lutheran Church in the United States has voted to repudiate Martin Luther's anti-Semitic teachings. Many Christians have recognized the devastating effects that the Crusades had on non-Christians' views of Jesus and his teachings, and many are also rediscovering Christianity's Jewish roots.

Day Five | Who Really Killed Jesus?

The Very Words of God

I am the good shepherd; I know my sheep and my sheep know me — just as the Father knows me and I know the Father — and I lay down my life for the sheep.... No one takes it from me, but I lay it down of my own accord. I have authority to lay it down and authority to take it up again.

John 10:14–18

Bible Discovery

Who Was Responsible for Jesus' Death?

As Jesus' trial progressed, some people in Jerusalem directed fierce rage and hatred toward him. When Pilate expressed his belief in Jesus' innocence and wanted to release him, the unruly mob reacted by accepting full responsibility for Jesus' death: "Let his blood be on us and on our children" (Matthew 27:25)! Since then, many Christians (the Crusaders among them) have blamed the Jews for killing Jesus. But did God place the blame for Jesus' death on that Jewish mob and their children? Did they represent and speak for all Jews?

1. In what way did many Jewish people respond to Jesus and his teaching? (See Mark 11:18; Luke 20:39.)

2. What made it difficult for the chief priests and other religious leaders to arrest Jesus and keep him from teaching? (See Matthew 26:3 – 5; Luke 19:47 – 48; 20:19; 22:1 – 6.)

3. Which people actually plotted against Jesus and had him arrested? Why did they do this? (See Luke 19:47; John 11:45 – 53; 18:12 – 14.)

   NOTE: Some, but not all, of the Pharisees and other religious leaders plotted against Jesus.

4. Which people actually were responsible for Jesus' ill treatment and execution? (See Matthew 27:11 – 14, 26 – 31; Luke 18:31 – 33; 23:13 – 25; John 19:16.)

5. As Jesus was being led away to be crucified, what did some of the people do? (See Luke 23:26 – 27.)

6. What was Jesus' attitude toward those who crucified him? (See Luke 23:34.)

7. In light of what God told Ezekiel about each person's responsibility regarding sin, who do you think God holds accountable for killing Jesus? (See Ezekiel 18:1 – 4, 19 – 20, 30.)

8. How did Paul, a Jew, who knew that some of his own people had supported Jesus' crucifixion, respond to other Jews, and what was his hope for them? (See Romans 10:1; 11 – 13; 11:1 – 5, 11.)

Reflection

More than just one group of people had a role in Jesus' death. The most important truth relating to Jesus' death, however, is not who accuses whom. The most important truth is found in understanding who Jesus is, why he came to earth, and the difference his death and resurrection continues to make. Several passages in the gospel of John help to clarify this: John 1:29; 3:16; 10:14 – 18.

For whom did Jesus die?

Who sent Jesus to die for the sins of the world?

Who decided that Jesus would give up his life as a sacrifice?

If each person is responsible before God for his or her own sin, and if Jesus willingly died as the sacrifice for the sin of every person, then who is ultimately responsible for Jesus' death?

How does this realization influence your relationship with Jesus? Your desire to serve him with all your heart, soul, and strength?

How does this realization influence your desire to break down stereotypes and relate to groups of people who have been wronged by Christians in the past?

Memorize

God demonstrates his own love for us in this: While we were still sinners, Christ died for us.

Romans 5:8

A TRAGIC HISTORY

c. AD 27–30	Jesus' ministry
66–73	First Jewish revolt against Rome
70	Rome destroys Jerusalem
131–135	Second Jewish revolt
315	Constantine forbids Jews from proselytizing
439	Jews denied the right to hold public office and build new synagogues
600	Pope Gregory forbids Jews from eating with Christians
613	Forced baptisms in Spain; Jews who refuse are expelled and their children under age seven are given to Christians
632	Byzantine emperor Heraclius I forces Jews to either be baptized or be killed
1075	Pope Gregory VII prohibits Jews from holding office in Christian countries
1096	First Crusade—Jewish and Muslim communities are slaughtered across Europe, Turkey, and Israel
1144	Second Crusade—mobs kill Jews throughout Europe
1170	Third Crusade—Jews are killed throughout Europe
1198	Pope Innocent III begins Fourth Crusade—Jews had to wear badges and were killed to atone for Jesus' death
1291	Crusaders leave Palestine
1320	Shepherds' Crusade—communities of Jews are slaughtered in Europe
1933–1945	Nazi Holocaust

LIVING WATER

Israel's mountains, rocky plateaus, deep wadis, and windswept deserts help to create a wilderness panorama of breathtaking beauty and insidious danger. Wadis flood suddenly. The desert sun beats down on creatures and plants that have adapted to the dry, scorching heat of the day and the chill of cloudless nights. In such inhospitable places, water is the one resource that enables the wilderness to support life.

People who lived in and near the desert lands of the Bible were painfully aware of their need for life-giving water. Perhaps that is one reason images of water are often mentioned in the Bible:

- The psalmist described how his soul thirsts for God "in a dry and weary land where there is no water" (Psalm 63:1). Elsewhere he wrote: "As the deer pants for streams of water, so my soul pants for you, O God" (Psalm 42:1).

- Biblical writers made a distinction between "living water" (meaning fresh, clean, pure, free-flowing water) and "cistern" or "dead" water (meaning stored water that may be stagnant and dirty).

- Jesus, too, spoke of the "living water" he could provide — water that would be like a spring of living water, welling up to eternal life (John 4).

- The prophet Jeremiah warned God's people against the incredible folly of forsaking God's living water and seeking their own water from broken cisterns!

These ancient images of the inhospitable wilderness and the living water that God freely gives to his people communicate an important message. Life is in many ways like living in the Judea Wilderness. It can be hot, dry, and barren, yet this is where we are called to live and accomplish God's work. The wilderness is the home of thirsty, hungry people who need Jesus' message and love. Living there, however, can sap our strength and make us weary of trying to serve God and reach out to others.

God — the giver of living water — understands our weariness. He knows what it's like to give to people until it hurts. He knows the heat … cold … loneliness … and dry emptiness that can come from living for Jesus in the wilderness. So God provides for his people places like En Gedi, an amazing oasis in the Judea Wilderness. Hardly more than a hundred feet or so from dry, rocky wilderness, water from the springs of En Gedi stream down from the rocks and support lush growth. For centuries, people in the wilderness have stopped at En Gedi to soothe their parched throats, water their animals, and gather the courage and strength to go back into the wilderness.

God encourages us to spend time daily refreshing ourselves in him. He is like our En Gedi. We need to read his Word, pray to him, listen for him, reflect on his truths with other Christians, and praise him. When we do that, it's like drinking living water — being refreshed amidst the desert's harsh heat, regaining strength when we are faint, and feeling spiritually alive again.

Will we seek God as our source of living water and refreshment? Or, will we vainly dig our own cisterns? Will we try to satisfy our spiritual thirst by chasing after things that cannot satisfy? Will we place our faith in our talents, hard work, friends, and success? Will we pursue things that look refreshing from a distance — like the Dead Sea — but have no life to give?

All such broken cisterns will fail us. Our ability to be effective Christians in a spiritually barren world comes from our loving, eternal, all-sustaining God. He is the Rock from whom streams of water flow. He freely gives "living" water to those who thirst. He is like an oasis that offers shade and "living," pure water. We can always come to him, be refreshed, and go back into the world with something to share with other people.

Opening Thoughts (4 minutes)

The Very Words of God

> *Jesus stood and said in a loud voice, "If anyone is thirsty, let him come to me and drink. Whoever believes in me, as the Scripture has said, streams of living water will flow from within him."*
>
> John 7:37–38

Think About It

Imagine that you live in a dry, drought-stricken region. As plants die and wells and reservoirs dry up, someone offers you and everyone else in the area all the pure, running water you need if you just ask for it. So, you ask every day and receive plenty of water. However, some people won't ask for water. Others don't seem to know that they have access to abundant water. So, they struggle to dig up the sun-baked ground in hopes of finding enough water to stay alive. How would you respond to these people?

DVD Teaching Notes (24 minutes)

Water in the wilderness—a spring of life

The "living water" of God

The "dead water" of our own cisterns

God as our oasis

DVD Discussion (7 minutes)

1. Find En Gedi on the map on page 267. Notice how close this oasis is to the Dead Sea (about a mile), how isolated it is from the civilization of the Judea Mountains, and how expansive the wilderness is from north to south. What would the abundant, rushing water of the En Gedi springs mean to people who traveled through this part of the wilderness?

2. At the oasis of En Gedi, lush, green plants thrive and streams of water rush down the rocks in what is otherwise a hot, dry, barren wilderness. In what ways have these images changed your understanding of what the Bible refers to as "living water" and "cistern water"?

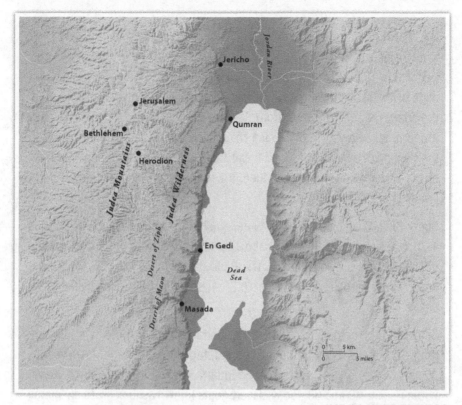

JUDEA WILDERNESS

3. After hiding from Saul in the wilderness, how do you think David and his men felt when they took refuge at En Gedi? How might it have affected them spiritually as well as physically?

4. When life in our world is challenging and demands all we have to give, much as life in the wilderness does, what does spending time with God each day provide for us? If you feel comfortable doing so, share with the group about a time when God refreshed you with an En Gedi–like experience.

DATA FILE
The Oasis of En Gedi

Sandwiched between the western shore of the Dead Sea and the eastern edge of the Judea Wilderness where it seldom rains, the springs of En Gedi provide a refreshing retreat from the barren, sun-baked heights that surround it. Miles away, in the Judea Mountains, rainfall seeps into cracks in the rock and flows underground toward En Gedi. A few hundred yards west of the waterfall shown in the video, those underground streams of water literally gush out from the rock.

Many Bible passages speak of water gushing from rock, such as Exodus 17:6, Deuteronomy 8:15, and Psalm 105:41. This adds to our understanding of God and his provision for us. The Bible describes God as the Rock from which water came (1 Corinthians 10:3–4; see also Deuteronomy 32:4, 31; Psalm 78:35).

Since En Gedi belonged to the tribe of Judah, David and his men hid from King Saul there. They no doubt appreciated its cool shade, lush beauty, pools and streams of water, and abundant wildlife. In this context, David wrote Psalms 42 and 63. Today, desert goats known as ibex graze on sparse grasses in the desert around En Gedi. Because they are so thirsty, they come to the oasis to drink even when people are nearby.

Small Group Bible Discovery and Discussion (14 minutes)

God Gives Living Water to Those Who Seek Him

Just as David and his men needed the life-giving water of En Gedi in order to survive in the wilderness, we also need the refreshment of God's pure, "living water" in order to serve him in the wilderness of life. When we are properly nourished and filled with his living water, we overflow with streams of living water; we have something to share with thirsty, needy people who live in a spiritually barren world. But in order to have anything to give, we need to have En Gedi moments — times of devotion, Bible study, prayer, retreat, meditation — when we meet with God and satisfy our spiritual thirst with his living water.

1. To what did God liken himself? (See Jeremiah 2:13; 17:13.)

    How desperately does God say we need what he provides for us?

2. Which images did David use to describe his need for God? (See Psalm 63:1.)

    Now that you have seen a few images of David's world — the barren wilderness, the heat, the lack of water, the abundance and beauty of the springs — how do you better understand his relationship with God?

3. What did Jesus say about the "living water" he came to give? (See John 4:13 – 14.)

4. At the end of Sukkot (Feast of Tabernacles), Jesus offered a bold invitation regarding living water. (See John 7:37 – 52.)

    a. What did he invite crowds of people to do, and what did he say would be the result?

b. What impact did his words have on various people who heard him? How thirsty were they? To what extent do you think they understood his message?

DATA FILE
The Feast of Sukkot

During Old Testament times, God instituted a religious calendar for the Israelites to follow. The seventh day, the seventh year, and the end of seven years were significant to him. Within each year, he specified seven feasts (Leviticus 23), one of which was the Feast of Sukkot (Tabernacles).

The celebration of Sukkot began after the fall harvest, a time to be especially thankful for God's blessings. It was a time to praise God for his past gifts of freedom, land, and bountiful harvests. In fact, God commanded them to "rejoice" before him (Leviticus 23:40). Following God's command, his people came to Jerusalem and built booths of olive, palm, and myrtle branches (Nehemiah 8:15) that provided shade. The people were to leave enough space in the branches so that they could see the sky, reminding them of their wilderness years. These booths (*sukkot,* plural *sukkah*) gave the feast its name. For seven days, the people ate, lived, and slept in these booths.

A special element of the celebration of Sukkot involved living water. Sukkot took place at the end of the dry season, so the rains needed to begin immediately to ensure a bountiful harvest the following year. Thus the celebration of God's harvest was coupled with the people's fervent prayers for the next year's rains. The priests, too, added a ceremony that included a prayer for rain. During this ceremony, a procession of priests marched from the temple to the Pool of Siloam, which was fed by the Spring of Gihon. One priest filled a golden pitcher with water, and the procession returned to the temple. At that time, the priest carrying the pitcher stood near the top of the altar and solemnly poured the water into one of two silver funnels leading into the stone altar for the daily drink offerings. At this time, the people — accompanied by the Levitical choir — began a chant that meant, "O Lord, save us by sending rain as well." In this way, they asked God for life-giving rain.

During Sukkot, four great menorahs (more than seventy-five feet high) were also placed in the women's court of the temple. They commemorated the miraculous burning of a small amount of sacred oil for eight days in the menorah (eternal light) in the Holy of Holies after Judah Maccabee defeated the Greek army of Antiochus and reclaimed Jerusalem.

In the context of Sukkot, the water ceremony, and the menorahs blazing with light, Jesus presented the message of his new kingdom. He had traveled to Jerusalem for Sukkot (John 7:10) and had taught great crowds thronging the temple (John 7:14). On the "last and greatest day of the Feast" (John 7:37), during the water ceremony, the chanted prayers, and the plea made through the offering of living water, Jesus stood and said, "If anyone is thirsty, let him come to me and drink. Whoever believes in me, as the Scripture has said, streams of living water will flow from within him" (John 7:37 – 38). So, the setting in which Jesus chose to give this lesson, and the similarity of his meaning to Jewish tradition, meant that his shouted promise in the temple must have had stunning impact: "Let him come to *me*!"

The Feast of Sukkot will be fully realized in heaven. There, God's people will experience living water (Revelation 7:17), his eternal presence (Revelation 21:22), and the light of God (Revelation 22:5). Whereas Sukkot taught the Jewish people to be joyful in anticipation of heaven, imagine the most joyful celebration that ever existed lasting for eternity. That, indeed, is heaven!

Faith Lesson (5 minutes)

Review the words from the song, "En Gedi," and reflect on how essential it is for you to receive God's living water every day.

Life is not so easy,
As a Christian standing stone.
It's a barren wilderness,
You can't make it on your own.
For work to be a good thing

You must face the dusty heat.
But you're called to find some rest,
Gaining strength to not be beat.
Do not dig a cistern,
Letting pleasures get ahead.
For the water you need clean,
Will be stale and dry instead.
But the waters of En Gedi,
Are fresh and flow with life.
So find the Lord in prayer,
Quench your thirst, and end your strife.
Oh, En Gedi, taking refuge in the Lord,
En Gedi, letting Jesus' words reward.
Drinking living water,
Resting in the shade.
Finding all the comfort,
To never be afraid.
En Gedi, a quiet peace with God.

Ben Lappenga

1. How does living in your culture (the desert wilderness) affect your desire for God (the oasis of En Gedi)?

2. In what ways has God been like the oasis of En Gedi for you, and how does that help you face the wilderness of life?

3. Where can you find an "En Gedi," a place where you can be restored through God's shade and living water, in the midst of your life?

4. Although it is tempting to stay at En Gedi — the refreshing oasis of God's presence — God calls you to live in a difficult world so that you can be his witness. How effectively are you reaching out to spiritually thirsty people in the wilderness of life?

Closing (1 minute)

Read together Psalm 52:8-9: "I am like an olive tree flourishing in the house of God; I trust in God's unfailing love for ever and ever. I will praise you forever for what you have done; in your name I will hope, for your name is good. I will praise you in the presence of your saints." Then pray, focusing on your need for God as you face each challenging day in the wilderness of life. Thank him for his love, kindness, and readiness to give you rest and to satisfy your deepest needs. Ask him to help you maintain a passionate faith and to remember to praise him for what he has done for you.

Memorize

> *I am like an olive tree flourishing in the house of God; I trust in God's unfailing love for ever and ever. I will praise you forever for what you have done; in your name I will hope, for your name is good. I will praise you in the presence of your saints.*
>
> *Psalm 52:8-9*

Understanding the World in Which Jesus Lived

In-Depth Personal Study Sessions

Day One | God Provides for His People

The Very Words of God

> *Surely, O LORD, you bless the righteous; you surround them with your favor as with a shield.*
>
>

Psalm 5:12

Bible Discovery

God Is Generous and Faithful in Meeting the Needs of His People

As the Jews faced the rigors of the wilderness on their way to the Promised Land, God met their needs. Although life in the desert wilderness was difficult, God was leading them to a better place — to a homeland that was just as beautiful and desirable as the fresh-water springs of En Gedi would be to a desert traveler. God has been and always will be faithful to provide for his people as they obediently serve him in the wilderness of life.

1.   How did God provide for the Israelites as they wandered in the wilderness, and why? (See Psalm 105:37 – 45.)

2.   What did God promise to do for the Israelites if they faithfully obeyed his commands, loved him, and served him devotedly? (See Deuteronomy 11:10 – 15; 28:1 – 13.)

How appealing would these images have been for people who were in a vast and barren desert?

How much do you desire this kind of provision from God?

3. What does Psalm 107:1 – 9 reveal about God's enduring love, his faithful provision, and how he wants us to respond to him?

4. What does God promise to do for those who wander in the desert, those whom God refers to as "the poor and needy" who "search for water"? Why does he do this? (See Isaiah 41:17 – 20.)

5. What eternal provision has God made for people who believe in him? (See Isaiah 35:6 – 10.)

In what ways is what God has promised like an oasis in the wilderness?

Reflection

God's care for the ancient Israelites demonstrated his faithfulness to them, and to everyone who belongs to him and remains obedient to him. No matter how rugged and desolate our wilderness is, we can always count on God to provide for us. May we always be thankful and eager to praise him for his goodness.

> Which specific needs in your life, or the life of someone you love, require God's intervention and provision?

> On a scale of one (low) to ten (high), how much are you trusting God to meet those needs?

> To what extent is there a difference in your confidence in God's provision during times of plenty in the oasis? During times of need in the wilderness?

How well do you remember God's provision for you — during times of need as well as during times of refreshment?

When we're feeling pressured by the challenges of the wilderness, our memory of God's goodness is often lacking. So it's important to put into place practices that will help us remember what God has done for us and praise him for it. That is part of the reason God instituted feasts and celebrations for Israel to follow — so they would always remember what he had done.

How might keeping a journal of these blessings help you to *remember* his provision for you in the past? If you do this, you may want to include vivid descriptions of what God has provided.

For which of God's provisions might it be appropriate to set up a "standing stone" in your yard as a memorial?

During which holiday or family gathering could you add a practice of remembrance, praise, or celebration for God's provision?

Memorize

> *Those who know your name will trust in you, for you, LORD, have never forsaken those who seek you. Sing praises to the LORD, enthroned in Zion; proclaim among the nations what he has done.*
>
> **Psalm 9:10 – 11**

Day Two | Our God — An "Oasis" in the Wilderness

The Very Words of God

> *Taste and see that the LORD is good; blessed is the man who takes refuge in him.... Those who seek the LORD lack no good thing.*
>
> **Psalm 34:8 – 10**

Bible Discovery

Come to God and Be Refreshed

Wilderness metaphors that the biblical writers used to describe God communicated powerfully to those who had experienced life as wanderers in the wilderness. Those metaphors have an important message for us as well. God wants us to come to him, as our "En Gedi," to be refreshed from the rigors of the wilderness. As we learn to see God as our "oasis" and ask him for help, he will respond with the "shade" and "living water" that restores us.

1. Life in the wilderness of daily life is often like being in the brutal heat of the desert sun. It dehydrates and exhausts us. In the context of wilderness living, how do the following verses help us see God as our oasis?

Scripture Text	God as Our Oasis
Ps. 61:1–4	
Ps. 91:1–2	
Ps. 121:5–8	
Isa. 25:4–5	

2. The Word of God helps to provide the refreshment and nourishment we need to not only survive but to thrive in the wilderness. What are some of the images the psalmist used to describe the Word of God? (See Psalms 19:9–11; 119:92–93, 102–103, 129–130.)

In what ways do these images portray God's Word as a much-needed oasis for the soul?

NOTE: Honey was the only naturally sweet substance ancient people had. As such, it was highly valued. The Bible describes God's blessings as being like honey.

3. Which imagery did Paul use to describe the Israelites' source of "living" water that quenched their spiritual thirst, and what do you think this means for us? (See 1 Corinthians 10:1 – 4.)

WATER FROM ROCK

4. Living in the "wilderness" of culture is where we learn to
    depend on God as we seek to fulfill his calling. What does
    God do for those who obey him and seek him? (See Isaiah
    58:11.)

5. What beautiful image did Jeremiah use to describe a person
    who trusts in God and his provision? (See Jeremiah 17:7 – 8.)
    In contrast, what happens when we trust in ourselves rather
    than in God? (See Jeremiah 17:5 – 6.)

Reflection

Every day, as we live in the wilderness of life, we have the opportunity to choose where we will place our trust and where we will
seek refreshment. Will we turn to God — or someone or something
else? It's a choice that makes all the difference.

> What were your thoughts as you read some of the scriptural
> images for God and how he wants to provide relief from the
> desert wilderness and bless, refresh, and nourish his people?

> How deeply do you long for what God gives to his people?

What obstacles keep you from drinking deeply of the good-ness God offers?

David described the Word of God using such terms as gold, honey, and light. Which words, based on your experiences with God in the desert and in the oasis, would you use to describe it?

What do you need to do to take refuge in God?

In what ways do you need to seek him as your source of life and ask him for help and strength?

What action will you take to go to the oasis and drink your fill of the living water God provides?

Memorize

The LORD will guide you always; he will satisfy your needs in a sun-scorched land and will strengthen your frame. You will be like a well-watered garden, like a spring whose waters never fail.

Isaiah 58:11

Day Three | Empty Substitutes for God's Living Water

The Very Words of God

Why spend money on what is not bread, and your labor on what does not satisfy? Listen, listen to me, and eat what is good, and your soul will delight in the richest of fare. Give ear and come to me; hear me, that your soul may live.

Isaiah 55:2–3

Bible Discovery

The Futility of Depending on Our Own Strength

Even though we know that God freely offers living water to those who seek him, we often chase after substitutes. Through our own strength and effort, we pursue success, pleasure, and fulfillment. But the Bible, the faithful and true Word of God, reveals what happens when we rely on our own strength and efforts in order to survive. Through story after story, warning after warning, we discover that without God even attractive and good things cannot satisfy our deepest needs and desires. Nothing but the living water of God can quench our spiritual thirst.

1. As you read the following Bible passages, notice the substitute for God's provision that is being sought and take note of the consequences and futility of such pursuits. Then look closely at your own heart and life and consider the ways in which you rely on your own strength and efforts to pursue the same things.

Scripture Text	Substitutes for God's Provision	Consequences and Futility of Such Pursuits for Others/for Me
Prov. 18:11; Luke 12:15–21; Rev. 3:17		

Scripture Text	Substitutes for God's Provision	Consequences and Futility of Such Pursuits for Others/for Me
Deut. 8:12–14; Ps. 10:2–4		
Eccl. 2:10; 6:7		
Eph. 4:1		
Ps. 40:4; Col. 3:5		

2. Even two of Israel's greatest kings fell into the trap of scorning what God offered and trying to meet their own needs in their own way.

   a. What did King Solomon choose to pursue instead of God, and what did he lose as a result? (See 1 Kings 11:1 – 11.)

   b. What terrible loss did King Uzziah, who had such great success in the eyes of God early in his life, suffer during the last years of his life? (See 2 Chronicles 26:3 – 21.)

Reflection

The Bible offers great wisdom to help you remain focused on God and his "living water" rather than trusting in yourself and seeking fulfillment from things that can never satisfy. Take some time right now to read the following three passages that capture the futility of pursuing our own desires in our own way: 1 John 2:15 – 17; 1 Timothy 6:17; Matthew 16:26.

What will happen to everything in the world that you desire?

What is the price of gaining what the world offers?

What consequences have you witnessed when people you know (or you yourself) have pursued substitutes for God?

In which area(s) do you still tend to pursue the empty rewards of this life rather than accepting the gift of God's life-giving provision?

What steps might you take to change the focus and direction of your pursuit?

Day Four | Living Water or Broken Cisterns —
The Choice Is Ours

The Very Words of God

> *My people have committed two sins: They have forsaken me, the spring of living water, and have dug their own cisterns, broken cisterns that cannot hold water.*
>
> *Jeremiah 2:13*

Bible Discovery

Our Best Efforts Cannot Save Us

Many things in our culture look as if they will provide living water, but they all fail to give abundant life or to satisfy our thirst for God. The Dead Sea, for example, looks refreshing from a distance, but its bitter saltwater cannot satisfy. It is equally foolish to turn our backs on God's pure, refreshing, life-giving water and try to dig our own cisterns, which — if they hold water at all — provide only dead, stagnant water. In the language of Scripture, trying to live without God is like turning away from the gushing, cool springs of En Gedi to seek dirty water from broken cisterns.

1. Psalm 107:4 – 9, 33 – 38 describes what God has done for his people.

   a. What was their condition before they turned to God?

   b. After they turned to God — their source of living water — what did he provide for them?

A BROKEN CISTERN

2.   Before the Israelites entered the Promised Land, what serious warning did God give to them, and why did he say it was
necessary? (See Deuteronomy 8:10 – 18.)

3.   Once they were settled in the Promised Land, which sins did
God's people commit? (See Jeremiah 2:13.)

In what ways do we do the same things today?

4. What is the tragedy of turning away from God and depending on our own cisterns? (See Jeremiah 14:1 – 3.)

5. In contrast to a person who has nothing to depend on but an empty cistern, what does a person who spends time in God's "oasis" — praying, reading and meditating on the Bible, worshiping, praising, obeying God — receive from God? (See Psalms 1:1 – 3; 91:2 – 4; 121:4 – 8.)

FACT FILE
What Was "Cistern Water"?

In Israel, the rainy season is only five months long, from November through March. Since fresh springs like those at En Gedi are rare, most ancient cities, towns, and households used cisterns to catch and store runoff from rooftops, courtyards, or even streets. So, cistern water wasn't like the clean, fresh, cool, flowing water of a spring. It was likely to be stale and dirty — perhaps even fouled by dead animals.

Furthermore, cisterns were dug by hand out of solid rock and were plastered so they would hold water. They needed constant care because the plaster tended to fall off, which allowed precious water to leak out. When a cistern failed to hold water, it created a desperate situation for everyone who depended on it.

Reflection

Many people today are determined to live without God. They turn their backs on what he freely gives only to become enslaved to labor in their own strength for what they can never achieve for themselves.

> When have you chosen a broken cistern over God's oasis where living water flows in abundance?

> What motivated you, and what did you hope to gain by making that choice?

> What did you receive for your efforts, and to what extent did it satisfy you?

> On the other hand, what price have you paid (or are you paying) for making that choice?

> What would you say to other people who are pursuing the same path you took? What choice would you encourage them to make?

How would you like God to meet your needs and satisfy your longings as you move ahead on your life's journey?

What are some ways you can spend time in the oasis of God's presence so that you will not just survive but thrive in the desert wilderness of life?

What are you doing to continually thank and praise God for what he — and he alone — provides for you?

Memorize

It is better to take refuge in the LORD than to trust in man. It is better to take refuge in the LORD than to trust in princes.

Psalm 118:8 – 9

DID YOU KNOW?
Cisterns Were Used for More Than Water!

Served as prisons	(Joseph) Genesis 37:21 – 28; (Jeremiah) Jeremiah 38:6 – 13
Were symbols of prosperity	2 Kings 18:28 – 32
Served as hiding places	1 Samuel 13:6
Used as tombs	Jeremiah 41:7 – 9
Built by kings as well as common people	2 Chronicles 26:9 – 10
Used in teaching metaphors	Proverbs 5:15 – 18

Day Five | Sharing God's Living Water

The Very Words of God

The fruit of the righteous is a tree of life, and he who wins souls is wise.

Proverbs 11:30

Bible Discovery

God's Living Water Gives Us Something to Share with Others

It's amazing to realize that God desires to use each of us to share his living water with other people. When we remain rooted in God and draw what we need from him rather than trying to obtain what we need through our own strength and efforts, we have the privilege of becoming fruitful members of God's kingdom. When we walk with him faithfully, we demonstrate the refreshing, healing nature of God's kingdom to people around us.

1. What incredible word picture does the Bible paint of a person who trusts fully in God and receives the living water he provides? (See Psalm 92:12 – 15.)

    What impact will such a person have in his or her culture?

2. As we take in our full measure of God's living water, what kind of "fruit" will we have to share with other people, according to the following passages?

    John 13:34 – 35

    Romans 15:13

    Galatians 5:22 – 25

    Ephesians 5:8 – 11

3. What essential actions must we take in order to keep receiving God's "living water" so that we can be fruitful and share what God has given us with other people? (See John 15:4 – 5; Colossians 2:6.)

Practically speaking, what does this involve in your life?

Reflection

God promises that his living water will flow through every Christian who follows him obediently. Imagine how families, neighborhoods, companies, communities, and even countries might change if each of us were to obey God passionately and bury our roots deep in the oasis of his presence! We have a great blessing and hope to share with the world. But we have nothing to share if we try to do it on our own. We need a right relationship with God and a humble heart that is willing to receive his instruction as well as the living water he offers.

Although it can be painful, what does God do in Christians' lives so that we may bear the best fruit? (See John 15:1 – 2; Hebrews 12:7 – 11.)

What does God need to prune out of your life so that you will be more fruitful?

In which areas are you being obedient to God? Being disobedient?

What specific things are you doing each day to cultivate a deeper relationship with God?

What price are you willing to pay to become more like Jesus so that his Spirit will flow through you freely?

What changes do you need to make in your heart and life in order to truly live out your commitment to share God's living water with people each day?

BIBLIOGRAPHY

History

Connolly, Peter. *Living in the Time of Jesus of Nazareth.* Tel Aviv: Steimatzky, 1983.

Ward, Kaari. *Jesus and His Times.* New York: Reader's Digest, 1987.

Whiston, William, trans. *The Works of Josephus: Complete and Unabridged.* Peabody, Mass.: Hendrikson Publishers, 1987.

Wood, Leon. Revised by David O'Brien. *A Survey of Israel's History.* Grand Rapids: Zondervan, 1986.

Jewish Roots of Christianity

Stern, David H. *Jewish New Testament Commentary.* Clarksville, Md.: Jewish New Testament Publications, 1992.

Wilson, Marvin R. *Our Father Abraham: Jewish Roots of the Christian Faith.* Grand Rapids: Eerdmans, 1986.

Young, Brad H. *Jesus the Jewish Theologian.* Peabody, Mass.: Hendrickson Publishers, 1995.

Geography

Beitzel, Barry J. *The Moody Atlas of Bible Lands.* Chicago: Moody Press, 1993.

Gardner, Joseph L. *Reader's Digest Atlas of the Bible.* New York: Reader's Digest, 1993.

General Background

Alexander, David, and Pat Alexander, eds. *Eerdmans' Handbook to the Bible.* Grand Rapids: Eerdmans, 1983.

Butler, Trent C., ed. *Holman Bible Dictionary.* Nashville: Holman Bible Publishers, 1991.

Edersheim, Alfred. *The Life and Times of Jesus the Messiah.* Peabody, Mass.: Hendrickson Publishers, 1994.

Archaeological Background

Charlesworth, James H. *Jesus Within Judaism: New Light from Exciting Archaeological Discoveries*. New York: Doubleday, 1988.

Finegan, Jack. *The Archaeology of the New Testament: The Life of Jesus and the Beginning of the Early Church*. Princeton: Princeton University Press, 1978.

Mazar, Amihai. *Archaeology of the Land of the Bible: 10,000 – 586 B.C.E.* New York: Doubleday, 1990.

To learn more about the specific backgrounds of this DVD series, consult the following resources:

Avigad, Nahman. "Jerusalem in Flames — The Burnt House Captures a Moment in Time." *Biblical Archaeology Review* (November–December 1983).

Barkey, Gabriel. "The Garden Tomb — Was Jesus Buried Here?" *Biblical Archaeology Review* (March–April 1986).

Ben Dov, Meir. "Herod's Mighty Temple Mount." *Biblical Archaeology Review* (November–December 1986).

Bivin, David. "The Miraculous Catch." *Jerusalem Perspective* (March–April 1992).

Burrell, Barbara, Kathryn Gleason, and Ehud Netzer. "Uncovering Herod's Seaside Palace." *Biblical Archaeology Review* (May–June 1993).

Edersheim, Alfred. *The Temple*. London: James Clarke & Co., 1959.

Edwards, William D., Wesley J. Gabel, and Floyd E. Hosmer. "On the Physical Death of Jesus Christ." *Journal of American Medical Association (JAMA)* (March 21, 1986).

Flusser, David. "To Bury Caiaphas, Not to Praise Him." *Jerusalem Perspective* (July-October 1991).

Greenhut, Zvi. "Burial Cave of the Caiaphas Family." *Biblical Archaeology Review* (September–October 1992).

Hareuveni, Nogah. *Nature in Our Biblical Heritage*. Kiryat Ono, Israel: Neot Kedumim, Ltd., 1980.

Hepper, F. Nigel. *Baker Encyclopedia of Bible Plants: Flowers and Trees, Fruits and Vegetables, Ecology*. Ed. by J. Gordon Melton. Grand Rapids: Baker, 1993.

"The 'High Priest' of the Jewish Quarter." *Biblical Archaeology Review* (May–June 1992).

Hirschfeld, Yizhar, and Giora Solar. "Sumptuous Roman Baths Uncovered Near Sea of Galilee." *Biblical Archaeology Review* (November–December 1984).

Hohlfelder, Robert L. "Caesarea Maritima: Herod the Great's City on the Sea." *National Geographic* (February 1987).

Holum, Kenneth G. *King Herod's Dream: Caesarea on the Sea.* New York: W. W. Norton, 1988.

Mazar, Benjamin. "Excavations Near Temple Mount Reveal Splendors of Herodian Jerusalem." *Biblical Archaeology Review* (July–August 1980).

Nun, Mendel. *Ancient Stone Anchors and Net Sinkers from the Sea of Galilee.* Israel: Kibbutz Ein Gev, 1993. (Also available from *Jerusalem Perspective.*)

_____. "Fish, Storms, and a Boat." *Jerusalem Perspective* (March–April 1990).

_____. "The Kingdom of Heaven Is Like a Seine." *Jerusalem Perspective* (November–December 1989).

_____. "Net Upon the Waters: Fish and Fishermen in Jesus' Time." *Biblical Archaeology Review* (November–December 1993).

_____. *The Sea of Galilee and Its Fishermen in the New Testament.* Israel: Kibbutz Ein Gev, 1993. (Also available from *Jerusalem Perspective.*)

Pileggi, David. "A Life on the Kinneret." *Jerusalem Perspective* (November–December 1989).

Pixner, Bargil. *With Jesus Through Galilee According to the Fifth Gospel.* Rosh Pina, Israel: Corazin Publishing, 1992.

Pope, Marvin, H. "Hosanna: What It Really Means." *Bible Review* (April 1988).

Riech, Ronny. "Ossuary Inscriptions from the Caiaphas Tomb." *Jerusalem Perspective* (July–October 1991).

_____. "Six Stone Water Jars." *Jerusalem Perspective* (July–September 1995).

Ritmeyer, Kathleen. "A Pilgrim's Journey." *Biblical Archaeology Review* (November-December 1989).

Ritmeyer, Kathleen, and Leen Ritmeyer. "Reconstructing Herod's Temple Mount in Jerusalem." *Biblical Archaeology Review* (November–December 1989).

_____. "Reconstructing the Triple Gate." *Biblical Archaeology Review* (November–December 1989).

Ritmeyer, Leen. "The Ark of the Covenant: Where It Stood in Solomon's Temple." *Biblical Archaeology Review* (January–February 1996).

_____. "Quarrying and Transporting Stones for Herod's Temple Mount." *Biblical Archaeology Review* (November–December 1989).

Ritmeyer, Leen, and Kathleen Ritmeyer. "Akeldama: Potter's Field of High Priest's Tomb." *Biblical Archaeology Review* (November–December 1994).

Sarna, Nahum M. *The JPS Torah Commentary: Exodus.* New York: Jewish Publication Society, 1991.

"Sea of Galilee Museum Opens Its Doors." *Jerusalem Perspective* (July–September 1995).

Shanks, Hershel. "Excavating in the Shadow of the Temple Mount." *Biblical Archaeology Review* (November–December 1986).

"Shavuot." *Encyclopedia Judaica,* Volume 14. Jerusalem: Keter Publishing House, 1980.

Stern, David. *Jewish New Testament Commentary.* Clarksville, Md.: Jewish New Testament Publications, 1992.

Taylor, Joan E. "The Garden of Gethsemane." *Biblical Archaeology Review* (July–August 1995).

Tzaferis, Vassilios. "Crucifixion — The Archaeological Evidence." *Biblical Archaeology Review* (January–February 1985).

_____. "A Pilgrimage to the Site of the Swine Miracle." *Biblical Archaeology Review* (March–April 1989).

_____. "Susita." *Biblical Archaeology Review* (September–October 1990).

Vann, Lindley. "Herod's Harbor Construction Recovered Underwater." *Biblical Archaeology Review* (May–June 1983).

More Great Resources
from Focus on the Family®

Volume 1: Promised Land

This volume focuses on the Old Testament—particularly on the nation of ancient Israel, God's purpose for His people, and why He placed them in the Promised Land.

Volume 2: Prophets and Kings of Israel

This volume looks into the nation of Israel during Old Testament times to understand how the people struggled with the call of God to be a seperate and holy nation.

Volume 3: Life and Ministry of the Messiah

This volume explores the life and teaching ministry of Jesus. Discover new insights about the Son of God.

Volume 4: Death and Resurrection of the Messiah

Witness the passion of the Messiah as He resolutely sets His face toward Jerusalem to suffer and die for His bride. Discover the thrill the disciples felt when they learned of His resurrection and were later filled with the Holy Spirit.

Volume 5: Early Church

Capture the fire of the early church in this fifth set of That the World May Know® film series. See how the first Christians lived out their faith with a passion that literally changed the world.

Volume 6: In the Dust of the Rabbi

"Follow the rabbi, drink in his words, and be covered with the dust of his feet," says the ancient Jewish proverb. Come discover how to follow Jesus as you walk with teacher and historian Ray Vander Laan through the breathtaking terrains of Israel and Turkey and explore what it really means to be a disciple.

Volume 7: Walk as Jesus Walked

Journey to Israel where the 12 disciples walked the walk their rabbi Jesus taught them. Examining the culture and the politics of the first century. Ray Vander Laan opens up the Gospels as never before.

FOR MORE INFORMATION

 Online:
Go to ThatTheWorldMayKnow.com

 Phone:
Call toll-free: 800-A-FAMILY (232-6459)
In Canada, call toll-free: 800-661-9800

Volume 8: God Heard Their Cry

Just when it seemed that Pharaoh could not be defeated, God provided for His People in ways they never could have imagined. Join historian Ray Vander Laan in ancient Egypt for his study of God's faithfulness to the Israelites—and promise that remains true today.

Volume 9: Fire on the Mountain

When the Israelites left Egypt, they were finally free. Free from persecution, free from oppression, and free to worship their own God. But with that freedom comes a new challenge—learning how to live together the way God intends. In this ninth set of That the World May Know® film series, discover how God teaches the Israelites what it means to be part of a community that loves Him, and the lessons we can begin to live out in our lives today.

Volume 10: With All Your Heart

Do you remember where your blessings come from? In Exodus, God warned Israel to remember Him when they left the dry desert and reached the fertile fields of the promised land. But in this tenth volume of That the World May Know® film series, discover how quickly the Israelites forgot God and began to rely on themselves.

Volume 11: The Path to the Cross

Discover how the Israelites' passionate faith prepares the way for Jesus and His ultimate act of obedience and sacrifice at the cross. Then, be challenged in your own life to live as they did by every word that comes from the mouth of God.

Volume 12: Walking With God in the Desert

Are you going through a difficult period of life? The loss of a loved one? Unemployment? A crisis of faith? During these desert times, it's easy to think God has disappeared. Instead, discover that it's only when we are totally dependent on Him that we find Him closer than ever and can experience God's amazing grace and provision.